Women like You and Me

By women like you and me

Copyright © Felicity Banner-Brown

The right of Felicity Banner-Brown to be identified as the compiler of this work is confirmed in accordance with the Copyright, Designs & Patents Act 1988.

All rights reserved. No copy, reproduction or transmission of this work, or part of this work, to include the cover illustration, may be made without written permission from the authors. Any person who does so may be liable to prosecution.

A CIP record catalogue of this book is available at the British Library.

~

The contents of this book have been collected from all over the world and in no way reflect any opinions, religions or any other controversial issue on any topic or at any level.

Profits from the sales of this book will go to charities for rape victims.

Danyelle Smith

Introduction

In aid of rape victims this book is a collection of stories by women and for women. The only thing the stories have in common is that they are all true. They vary from travel or parenting stories, to a traumatic story of rape, of illness, major trauma with children, and adventure.

After centuries of being considered weak, and even unworthy, women now feel free to show their muscle. And how strong we are!

We are the women of today. We are nothing like the women of our grandmother's worlds, nor like women for many centuries before. The lives we lead and the way we cope is a whole different ball game. Our horizons are far broader and, whether we are living through bad times or happy times, we share our stories with each other.

And, as we read, let us remember all those women who still live under archaic and unfair rules, under oppression or with ignorant husbands and fathers. It is the duty of all of us who are free write our stories to reach out to those who may … eventually …. one day … bring about change.

This book has no political message. It is just what it says it is: a collection of true stories from the women of today.

- Felicity Banner-Brown

Mark Scrivener

Contents by:

Abigail Paul

Anabel Lamshire

Balcita Blue

Carly Jim

Carol Lintott

Carol Scholes

Catherine Broughton

Cheryl Rowland-Nunez

Elizabeth Bailey

Felicity Banner-Brown

Jess Twitchin

Jinju

Martha Montour

Mary Hutton

Nadene Rose

Nicky Clifford

Moira Trill

Rita Miller

Teija de Vere

"A girl should be two things: classy and fabulous."

- *Coco Chanel*

Illustrations by:

Carol Scholes
Twitter: @CarolScholes
LinkedIn: Carol Scholes

Catherine Broughton
turquoisemoon.co.uk
seasidefrance.com

Daryl Tipping
theartgallery.co.uk

David Bailey

Felicity Banner-Brown

Frances Black, Marion Sweet, Ouna Black
berrylaneart.com
FB: Berry lane art group

Mandy Broughton
broughtonart.com

Mark Scrivener
mark-scrivener.blogspot.com

Kirsteen Lyons
createadrawingaday.blogspot.co.uk

Merrill Plowman

Editor's note – the illustrations are merely to add interest, not to illustrate the stories.

There's Wisdom in Women

"Oh love is fair, and love is rare;" my dear one she said,
"But love goes lightly over." I bowed her foolish head,
And kissed her hair and laughed at her. Such a child was she;
So new to love, so true to love, and she spoke so bitterly.

But there's wisdom in women, of more than they have known,
And thoughts go blowing through them, are wiser than their own,
Or how should my dear one, being ignorant and young,
Have cried on love so bitterly, with so true a tongue?

Rupert Brooke (1887-1915)

Marion Sweet

Dedicated to us,
by us.

Profits from the sales of this book will go to charities for rape victims.

Kirsteen Lyons

My Other Life

From Rita Miller, Africa

Biography: Rita Miller is Maltese and has lived in England, with her lawyer husband Paul, since 1979. They have a daughter, Julia. After qualifying as a registered nurse in 1984, Rita has worked both in primary and secondary care, laterally in general practice. She divides her time between Uganda and York, UK!

www.ritafrica.wordpress.com

I blame the Vicar of Dibley. That was the start.

A comedy programme, about the trials and tribulations of a female vicar's life in a rural Oxfordshire village, was to turn my life and that of my family upside-down.

Like many of us, I have watched numerous heart-breaking scenes on TV where healthcare in the developing countries would be stretched and aid workers battle with limited resources to overcome horrific epidemic or natural disaster. Many times I would wonder how on earth I could help, if at all, and I would end up switching off the TV or radio, in frustration and sadness.

I would dip in my pocket and give and hope that that money would end up where I wish it to be directed… and feel frustrated and sad.
Then the 1st January 2005 episode of the Vicar of Dibley, happened, It included a short video which apparently promoted the Make Poverty History Campaign. It was taken from a documentary called 'Orphans of Nkandala' and showed a brother and sister whose mother had died the previous year of Aids and the father too was now dying. Seeing this video was the defining moment: I thought enough was enough - as a nurse of over 30 years' experience I do possess the ability and skills to be of some use; so why not do something about it?

However it wasn't till five years later that the opportunity arose. After much planning and deliberating where in the world I would go, Kagando Hospital in Uganda, found me. It's an incredible story of how that happened – suffice to say that I felt someone, somewhere was pointing me in that direction. I could not ignore this.

January 2010 was my first visit to Kagando hospital, I went with another friend, Christine Pfluger, both of us nurse practitioners working in general practice in York. Following a couple of two week visits that year, I took a three month sabbatical from work, to go back to the hospital, and get the place 'out of my system'.

That plan failed abysmally. By the end of 2011 I had resigned from my job and since 2012 I go to Uganda on a 3monthly rota basis.
On my first trip to Kagando I had kept a kind of diary. The blogs came much later. I jotted thoughts and information, whatever came to mind. The following are two of those jottings:

Journey to Kagando: Day One

Excitement mounts as finally in Africa…1001 wishes before you die – one dream, to be part of Aid work in a Third World Country. No mustn't call it that now, not politically correct…Developing Country, that's what it is. Who decided on that title? Some officious bureaucrat in his (sexist?) soul-less office, void of feelings. Mind, not that I warm to the title of third world either. I wonder if these people have ever stepped outside their cocoon, and since when has it been developing – and who am I to be judge of that, or anything else for that matter? Santo Cielo, just because I've come to Africa, doesn't mean I suddenly turn into some pious authority; you should know better Rita.

The bureaucrat is so right. Here in Kampala I see shiny new buildings, buzzing with bustle and business. Ah no wait, sadly it's just a distraction. The poverty is there, weaving itself through prosperity as a permanent reminder of its Third World status…one, two, three: Oh, I see it now, it

all makes sense that word developing... the Government is absolving itself from the accountability of poverty because their country is still developing. I wonder if there is a time limit to such a title. When will the word stop having an 'ing' instead of an 'ed'... ah cynical me. I probably got it all wrong as per usual. I can hear my father say 'you and your rebellious thoughts'...Me, I prefer the word challenging.
Who am I? That's a good one; or rather Why am I me and not that man we've just passed, sitting on a stool outside his shack looking into where, thinking of what. What dreams does he hold I wonder, or are they long, long gone?

See that woman walking by roadside? She looks old beyond her years, carrying a child on her back. She's wearing a long patterned dress. It must have been beautiful once, those bright colours magnified, capturing the sunlight, cool despite the heat. Now the colours faded, weary and worn just like its owner. She looks so hot, the child still, the heat intense bouncing mirages on the uneven tarmac.

I take a sip of water from the bottle; I'm so glad I'm in the jeep with its AC cool interior, water... my excitement is wavering into a deep unease: why am I me and not that woman...who decides the so called lottery of birth? I turn to Chris to ask for her thoughts, maybe even for some reassurance, but I don't say anything – she knows.

A Rural Clinic

The green lush surroundings seem to magically disappear as we climb further into this hilly terrain. Nothing magical about this bumpy road; the battered car revving dust as it complainingly makes its way to the health clinic. No luxury of AC this time; I can taste the tacky dry air on my tongue. It's a good clinic I was informed; they rarely run out of drugs. We finally reach the tiny village and the car stops in front of a small building – a child plays with a few stones under the shade of a nearby tree. A box had been nailed to the tree 'suggestion box' written across it. We are greeted by the resident nurse and she invites us proudly into the clinic. Two steps, just two steps that's all it took before the stifling air hit me – the nurse's white starched uniform clashing with the oppressive interior. I wanted to turn back to the security of the outside, but how dare I do that? This is reality Rita not the comfort of your large consulting room, cool and airy with beautiful views across the lake. I willed myself back to the now, realising only too late that I had this fixed smile whilst the nurse was explaining how they managed to cope without electricity and water.

Oh stupid me.

My mind now in turmoil, rapidly trying to visualise what it is like to work here. I followed as she opened another door. 'We have a small ward in this clinic. Five beds, not enough if there is a malaria outbreak.'

They say you can smell fear. It was illness and hopelessness that greeted me: body odour and urine, infection mingling in the air. A far cry from the smells of cinnamon and orange candles that I had lit with abundance over the Christmas period. Was it only last week? I hold my breath. Breathe Rita, you must breathe, these people are living here. What exempts you from breathing their fetid air?

It took a few more seconds for my eyes to adjust to the semi darkness: then I saw the women and children; five women and three children to be precise – I felt my heart ache, it was a physical pain. I felt pain. Then I heard the stillness. I could not comprehend. I kept thinking no one is making a noise; there is no sound. The little ones just sitting there, please shout, cry, anything, just make a noise. The women look me at me, expectantly, with hope, – and almost instantly realising I have nothing to offer. In their eyes I see that look of resignation that I had to come to know so well this past week. And I feel impotent and ashamed of being me. How dare I be here? What can I do for these people? I don't blame them if they hate me; if they resent my presence. A little girl comes towards me and there is a tentative smile. I kneel down and look at the mother. I want her permission to hold the child – I hug her. It is I who need comfort. Oh God please help me, but where is God here, what good is my Faith to these people? I am so so angry. How can anyone let this happen? My Faith my God. There is no God, He cannot be.

A woman, her bed the mattress on the floor beckons to the nurse, she crouches down near her; they exchange quiet words in a language I do not understand. Nothing is making sense here. The woman grasps the nurse's hands and gently brings them to her forehead, slightly bowing her head as they make contact. I see the nurse, her white uniform no longer alien but somehow bringing comfort to this bleak room -and Faith is restored. God is here. We cannot blame God for humanities' failings. I want to be that nurse.

Why am I me, who am I? What can I tell this amazing nurse that would make her job, her life easier? What can I tell these women that would ease their pain give them hope, restore their dignity? All those questions are making my head hurt, not a migraine, no not here, not today. I step outside and take a deep breath. The suggestion box catches my eye. The irony of it all, Developing country? Nowhere near. Shame on all you Global Governments. I will return. I need to be accountable as well. I hate my conscience.

On the 5th June I wrote my latest blog; it is one of hope:

Meeting Rosie

A week before I was due to return to the UK, I was asked to visit a girl called Rosie. I was told she was blind and had other disabilities, and there were concerns that she was also malnourished. I went to see her with Sr Evanisa, a very experienced paediatric nurse (she is the in-charge of paediatrics and also lead nurse for Rwenzori Women for Health).

We found Rosie sitting on the floor in one of the two rooms of the house; a 15 yr old but in a child's body, eyes a distant look, yet when we spoke to her she smiled and turned her head to where she could her our voices. Although she was painfully thin we were relieved to see that there were no worrying signs of malnutrition. We had a long chat with her mother (sole carer) and we could see she did what she could for Rosie, with the little she had, but it was obvious they were poor.

The only item of 'furniture' in the room was a wheelchair. Someone had very kindly made Rosie a wheelchair from a plastic chair attaching four wheels to it; it worked but sadly it was far too big for her and she couldn't sit in it for any length of time as it was uncomfortable and she slid off it.

The situation broke my heart and I started to think what, if anything, could be done.

On returning to the hospital I spoke to Ken the physiotherapist – he said he would organise a wheelchair for Rosie. The wheelchairs available are provided by 'wheelchairs for kids Australia', they're brightly coloured and are fitted to the individual measurements...perfect!

Ken, Richard the technician, and I went back a couple of days later. I took with me some clothes, and toys including an activity toy, which I thought would be good for Rosie as it was tactile and noisy! I was given this toy some 3yrs ago but I kept it, waiting to hand it over to the right little person. So many times I'm given clothing, or toys, and I hold back until I think yes that's just right for that person – and so it proved to be...

As I held Rosie's hands over the toy and guided her to move wheels and cogs and made lots of noise, she proved to be a quick learner. I soon left her to it and started taking photos.

I was merrily clicking away, when I noticed Rosie had pulled the toy to her face and was very still. Uncertain what she was up to I lowered the camera to take a better look. She had found the mirror that was part of the activity toy! In an instant I realised what had happened, and before all emotions completely took over, I took some more photos until the moment I saw her raise her head and smile. It was all too much.

Rosie could see. It was a priceless experience.
The next day I arranged for Michael the clinical officer from the eye department, and William, another staff member to visit her, and more great news was to follow: they felt something could possibly be done to improve her sight…so watch this space!

As I look back on my blogs I reflect on the incredible six year journey so far. One that at my time of life I never envisaged would happen. This road has been a steep learning curve together with huge mixed emotions, from great joys to desperate heartache, always being prepared to expect the unexpected. A time of new discoveries, new beginnings an indulgence of experiences of sights sounds and smells, from a beautiful country with beautiful people.

This could never happen without the amazing support of my husband, Paul, our daughter Julia, the rest of my family and friends from UK, Malta and elsewhere who are always there for me.
My other Life….What a God-given privilege.

David Bailey

Abused women in Kurdistan

By Abigail Paul

This eye-opening and shocking piece comes to us anonymously, for obvious reasons. Calling herself Abigail Paul, this writer is a woman who has spent many years in third-world countries, battling injustices against women.

When I first moved to Kurdistan, Iraq, for work, there was some confusion and maybe some concern among my family and friends about my decision.

For many, just mentioning "Iraq" triggers an emotional reaction and conjures up images, stereotypes, and fears. When I first began considering a job managing a gender-based violence program for an international humanitarian organization in Kurdistan, I had conflicting thoughts, but I knew I wanted to work in a place where women and girls are most vulnerable and where I could put my experience and skills to good use.

Kurdistan is the semi-autonomous region in northern Iraq. It's important to understand that most Kurds do not identify as "Iraqis" and they are clear to distinguish themselves from Arab Iraqis who are mostly located in central (Baghdad) and southern Iraq. Many Kurds express fondness towards America. In 1991 the US created a "No Fly Zone" in northern Iraq, which provided relief from Saddam Hussein's horrific attacks on the Kurdish people. This area in northern Iraq is now known as Kurdistan. Many Kurds will tell you that they love George W. Bush and that he is their hero. In the words of some Kurds I have talked to, "George W. Bush gave us our freedom" or "America liberated us". So, while the US invasion of Iraq was extremely unpopular around the world, some Kurds have a different perspective.

The focus of my job here is to work with a variety of partners to develop strategies to protect the rights of women and girls, and to develop programs to prevent and respond to gender-based violence.

When I first arrived in KRI, I thought for sure I would start a blog, but things became intense very quickly, and it's been not only hard for me to find the time, but hard to find the words to describe my experience. To be honest, I have struggled here, and every day I struggle to stay. It's really bothered me that I haven't been able to write/blog/document what I'm seeing and experiencing, so I appreciate the opportunity to connect in some way to the rest of the world about my small place in this extremely complicated part of the world. Maybe someday I will write more, but for now, I will share a few thoughts.

There are many contradictions here in political, social, and religious life; it's confusing. On the surface, Kurdistan appears to be very different from central and southern Iraq, but with the work that I do, I see the "underbelly" of the culture and society here; I get to see the darker side of Kurdistan that is not always presented to the rest of the world. Kurdistan describes itself as a "free" society and one of the more progressive regions in the Middle East. It also prides itself on tradition, which is not great for women and girls in this context because it's mostly tradition, even more so than religion, that causes the most harm to women and girls.

To be clear, women and girls are not free here. This is a religious society with strong traditional and societal norms that can be extremely harmful to women and girls, including honour-based violence and honour-killings; coerced suicide (mostly by burning); female-genital mutilation; forced marriage; child marriage; isolation in homes; and sexual assault and rape. Honour-based violence, including honour killing, is common here and occurs when a woman or girl brings "shame" to her family, and the family or community decides that the only way that honour can be restored to the family is to kill the woman or girl. Or, the family or community coerces the woman or girl to commit suicide, often by burning, in order to cleanse and restore honour to the family.

One example of how a woman can bring shame to her family is to talk on a cell phone to a male who is not her husband or family member.

Rape survivors are often forced to marry their rapists to restore this so-called family honour. In addition, the law includes provisions for the perpetrator in that if he agrees to marry the woman or girl that he raped, he receives minimal penalty for his crime.

The government has passed some important legislation in recent years, including the Family Violence Law in 2011, which includes some provisions to protect women and girls. However, these laws are not being implemented, and international legal experts say that due to the many contradictions within the law itself and with the Constitution and other laws, it is impossible to implement; the law leaves too much room for interpretation, allowing the personal, cultural, and religious beliefs of judicial officials and tribal leaders to guide their decisions when faced with reports of honour-killings and other forms of gender-based violence. While these legislative efforts are encouraging on the surface, the laws are flawed and impossible to enforce as written.

I believe Kurdistan is moving through some difficult cultural and political changes; it wants to be a free and progressive society while holding onto to traditional norms that are harmful to women and girls. In there lies a conflict. A society cannot be truly free until all people enjoy equal rights, are living lives free of oppression and violence, and have equal access to resources. That goes for you too, America.

Do I feel like I've made any significant contribution to protecting the rights of women and girls? Most days, I do not. Some days, I do. I have some great Kurdish co-workers who are committed to improving the status of women and girls in Kurdistan. I am grateful for this. The progress is slow and sometimes invisible, and there are many discouraging moments. It will be interesting to see how Kurdistan deals with this dichotomy of tradition and progress in the coming years. I will always keep one eye on Kurdistan, no matter where I am in the world. Some places just leave a mark.

Ouna Black

Your footprint on my heart

From Nadene Rose, USA.

An hour a day with a Psychologist is never enough, I think it is a trick to us patients.

They bring us to the brink of a truth then casually remind us that our time has ended and we will pick up again the next time where we left off. , may in fact go about your life having these hour long talks with six or seven more people that day, but OUR talk is going follow me around till we see one another again. I am going to stew over all we talked about. I am going to get angry when I realize that you left me to figure this out on my own. I am going to burst into tears in front of others who are having a dandy conversation and they won't know what they have said or done to offend me.

Yes, you hold the map to my future and you are holding it out like a game of *What's behind door #1 "*
I will swing from total unfiltered anger one day to trusting you with the garbage I have told to no one but you. I will whine one day at the crappy way the world has treated me, and next take responsibility for my errors in judgement.

You my dear therapist will become mommy, daddy, friend, sister, brother, mentor and educator all in one. You will become the closest thing visible in my world. And you will have to walk alongside of me and be able to discern the difference between anger that is brought on by pain and needs a hug of validation and anger that is brought on by pity that needs a stern, loud voice of reason. You will have to hear ugly stories of painful abuse, and you will have to remain the calming voice.
You shall not ever get emotionally involved. As tempting as that may seem, save your emotional boundaries for that long cool drink at the end of the day when you close the curtains in your own home in order to stabilize your mind from the images I and others have placed on you for safe keeping.

I cannot ever witness your weakness, or my fear will indeed return. Give me the truth, for I need that to become whole but wait on showing me your weakness, for surely I will return to the land of lost and fearful souls.

And this my dear therapist is only the beginning, there is much work to do and there will be times I will give up, toss my heart and hands in the air and say, *"Forget it, I cannot do this anymore."* You will have to tell me, with honesty, that I am co-dependent. I will need to honestly admit that I am, but it will be one of the hardest things to admit.
You will need to convince me that throwing me out into the lawn head first breaking my arm in two places is not love but control. You will then need to convince me that I must file an abuse report on this incident, no one need know, it will be our little secrete, but you will validate that this indeed happened as you have the x-rays as proof. Or that the molestation I experienced was not my fault. And the day would come in the distance when I would thank you for this, I need only trust you, just this moment, as the pen signs my name.

The most empowering thing you will teach me is that, *"No is a good word!"* You will teach me appropriate responses, you will teach me how to heal my inner child, you will teach me visualization, and show me how to find the 'yellow light' of warning in my head when I am feeling threatened.

You will teach me how my victim mentality attracts predators.
You will teach me that indeed 'A Crime against A Child Has No Equal'. The damaged I sustained in growing up, while subtle, has had debilitating effects on my self-esteem, impaired personal relationships, and has severally limited my vocational skills.

I will never, ever forget you and your footprint remains on my heart to this day.

Frances Black

"Any woman who understands the problems of running a home will be nearer to understanding the problems of running a country."

- Margaret Thatcher

A Mother's Reflex: The Day I Became a Mother
From Jinju S. India

On 27th August 2015, I went to hell and back. But I emerged with a little bit of heaven in my arms—a pink, crinkled, swaddled, yawning bit of heaven that permeated cuteness from every pore. Words cannot describe the joy, pride and tenderness that swelled my heart in that ineffably magical moment when the nurse handed over to me a sleeping bundle of joy with a bracelet around his wrist that read 'Baby of Jinju'. So, literally speaking, that was the day I became a mother. Only that this phase of motherly euphoria was not to last long.

Thoroughly worn out by my arduous seventeen-hour-long labour and not having shut an eye for thirty six hours straight, all I wanted to do was draw the shades, grab a blanket and sleep undisturbed for the next twelve hours. Or at least the next six. But that day I realized that something as basic as sleep would henceforth be dictated by complex and unfathomable permutations and combinations of various factors that make up the crazy experience called new motherhood.

With an unceasing flow of excited relatives and visitors, not to mention a baby that would wake up and start crying to be fed every two hours with clockwork-like-regularity, I could not even nap properly. And to make things worse, postnatal aches set in with a vengeance after a few hours: every single fibre in my body was on fire, my muscles felt tender all over, the joints in my legs and hips were floating around. I couldn't climb onto the hospital bed, dress and undress or even lift my baby without squirming in pain. The sheen of motherhood had started wearing thin.

My baby hadn't yet learned to latch on properly and when my nipples cracked as a result, it was the last straw. That marked the beginning of my crying spells. I silently shed tears while nursing my baby on my sore breasts. I cried while taking a bath. I cried in the washroom. I cried and asked my mother and my aunt who were staying with me in the hospital why God was punishing me so much for delivering a baby! I was in the hospital for four days after my delivery and many a time during that harrowing period, I was racked with self-pity and doubt. I was no longer sure this was what I wanted in life. I felt guilty for my selfish thoughts. I wondered if I would be a good mother.

And then, on the day that I was to be discharged from the hospital, a nurse informed us that a lab report showed my baby was at a risk of developing neonatal jaundice and needed phototherapy. The intimidating phototherapy unit was brought into our room and after setting it up and giving us instructions to keep my baby under the lights for the next twelve hours with as few interruptions as possible, the hospital staff left. Even though the nurses had reassured me that this was nothing serious, I felt scared and depressed. The baby had to be suckled to sleep and then put underneath the lights with only his diaper and his eye shades on; we were also to ensure he didn't fidget with the goggles as the light could harm his eyes.

After three unsuccessful attempts—when placed under the lights, my baby would wake up with a start and scream his lungs out until he was picked up—my husband and I somehow managed to lay him in the plastic crib of the phototherapy unit without awakening him. I dragged myself onto the bed and leaned back into the pillows with a heavy sigh, asking my husband to stand beside the crib and keep an eye on our sleeping son. The room was full of people—my in-laws had arrived, along with a couple of visitors—and I forced myself to smile and interact with them.

Everything went fine for about ten minutes. And then it happened. My baby pulled off his eye shades and blinked. What happened next, I cannot clearly recount. Because before I knew it, I had flung myself over the crib with a piercing scream, trying to shield my baby's eyes from the light. I vaguely registered people shuffling urgently, my ribs clanging against the bed's metal rail, my father scrambling to switch off the phototherapy lights and the plastic of the crib cutting into my arms.

And then the lights were off and my husband picked up the baby. All of this happened in the flash of an eye. As I groaningly collapsed back into the bed, my heart racing, my back and shoulders aching from the sudden exertion, I saw that everyone in the room was staring at me in amazement. My father started berating me for throwing myself off my bed like that, explaining that only prolonged exposure to the light could harm my baby's eyes. I myself was lost for words. I did not know what had caused me to react that way. But I did know that it was instantaneous and I had not reasoned or thought for a moment. Flinging myself from the bed, I had draped myself over my baby before my husband who was standing right next to the crib could even move a finger, before my father could switch off the lights. And then one of the visitors, a Professor who had taught me in college, smiled and said softly, "Now that's what I would call a mother's reflex."

My baby and I were discharged the next day, after an exhausting night of taking turns in supervising the baby inside the phototherapy unit (and without further mishaps). It took my body over three months to recover completely from the after-effects of childbirth. During this period of recuperation, I continued having my ups and downs, but with each passing day, I regained a bit more of my physical strength and mental poise and bonded further with my baby. Now my son is a blooming five-month-old and I don motherhood like a second skin.

But the phototherapy mishap remains etched in my memory. Because that was when it struck me that this tiny, fragile, soul-rendingly hapless little human had plucked out my heart in a way that no one else had been able to so far, and would keep it in his tight clutch forevermore. And that was the day I realized I had truly become a mother.

Bio

Jinju S. is an Assistant Professor of English at a college in Kerala, India and a Doctoral Candidate in English Literature at the English and

Foreign Languages University, Hyderabad, India. Her life is an everyday struggle to juggle teaching, research, reading and writing with the most demanding and yet most rewarding journey of motherhood. She loves reading, writing poetry and short fiction, playing with her son Jizan, deep conversations, travelling to new places and listening to music. She blogs at jinjusoulspeak.blogspot.com

Maureen Molloy

I know God won't give me anything I can't handle. I just wish He didn't trust me so much.

- *Mother Teresa*

Catherine Broughton

I Never Saw it Coming

Elizabeth Bailey

The statistics are scary, but it's never going to happen to you. I bet most of us have a tendency to think "CANCER!" the moment there's anything wrong with the body. But deep down, you know it won't be that. Well, let me tell you, when it IS cancer, you don't believe it either.

I thought I'd just developed a little tummy. Hell, I was in my late sixties, what did I expect? Until I noticed the tummy consisted of hard lumps. Even then, I thought – "nah, it's muscles toughening up from the core exercises". Wrong. I had the sense to check with my exercise class teacher, who put an instant veto on that one.

"You haven't been for about three weeks. Muscles weaken if you don't keep it up."

That's when the alarm bells went off. I went to see my alternative practitioner – always my first port of call when the body goes wrong.
"If it's tumours," he said, "the body won't tell us. The body thinks tumours are just part of the body, so it doesn't react to testing."

Oh, great. I bit the bullet and opened investigations. Things happened fast after that. My doctor suspected an ovarian cyst, already the size of an orange. Malignant? Who knew? Whatever, it would mean an operation.

By this time, I was facing up to the truth. The likelihood was I had cancer. Time to tell the family.

I was living with my mother who had dementia, so I needed to arrange care while I was in hospital and for however many weeks it took to recover. I told my siblings. They took it well – we are all Scientologists and strong in dealing with life's crises - but at my request we kept it low profile until I knew what we were dealing with. A white lie that it was my niece having investigations (and me going in support instead of the other way round) saved my mother getting upset.

First off came an ultra sound, and that's when reality hit. Four masses? Not just the orange in the ovary? Now I was in trouble! I was outwardly calm, but I felt the shock hit. I sat in the car for a while, just looking at things outside while I processed the news because I didn't dare drive straight away.
As soon as I got home, I hit google. The best I could come up with was Stage 3 Ovarian Cancer. OK, so what do we do?

The one thing I knew was that no matter what, I was NOT having chemo or radiotherapy. I'd seen enough of what it did to bodies and I wasn't putting myself through that. Let's see about alternatives, shall we? I located ESSIAC, which seemed to me the best and simplest remedy. I resolved to order a course the moment I had a diagnosis.

Next up, the gynaecologist at Haywards Heath. I tell you the worst thing. No medico will EVER give you a "possible" diagnosis. They won't commit themselves until they actually know. You can't blame them, but it's tough when you are desperate for information. Their examination, though, indicated a lump over on the left side I hadn't known about. What the hell kind of cancer was this?

Back the following week for a CT scan – the first of many, for it's the number one check they have to make all the way along the line. That resulted in a referral to the Oncology Department at Brighton. Not ovarian then. Definitely cancer though.

At last I got a diagnosis. Try this on for size: Retroperitoneal Liposarcoma. Yes, I said the same: What the heck is that? It's extremely rare – about 250 people in the country present with it in a year as opposed to some 60,000 with breast cancer, for example.

The simple explanation: the peritoneum is a membrane that surrounds the abdominal organs. Lipo means fat. Sarcoma grows inside the cell as opposed to cancer which grows on the surface. Retro means behind. So this was a sarcoma that grew behind the peritoneum within the fat cells. The thing had pushed into the abdominal cavity from the left side, gone down into the lower part and up hard against my diaphragm and was creeping across to the right by the time I felt the lumps. I saw the scan on a monitor and couldn't believe my eyes. This thing was everywhere! What's more, it had destroyed my left kidney and possibly parts of other organs.

Brighton weren't sure of getting it all, so they referred me to the surgeons at the Royal Marsden in Chelsea. The Marsden is a specialist cancer hospital, with the result that we patients are all in the same boat and that makes for great solidarity and mutual support. I made good friends while I was there with whoever was in my ward at any time.
But back to my surgeon, who was one of the three top sarcoma specialists in the country. I adored him from the off. His statement gave me the first moment of belief that I might get through this thing.
"We can't use chemo because it doesn't work on this particular type of sarcoma. We can't use radiotherapy because there are too many organs in the way. So we will operate and remove the whole thing and you can resume a normal life."

Phew! The operation was arranged for about 9 days before Christmas and he said if I was lucky and all went smoothly, I might be out in time. I wasn't, but that was to come.

I spent hours in the hospital that day, going through all the pre-op preps, seeing the anaesthetist, getting weighed, you name it. It got more real by the minute. And by this time, I was starting to get tired and finding it hard to walk around because my tummy was growing like there's no tomorrow, though the rest of me was losing weight as the cancer took over. I began to look pregnant – not a good look at my age. The diagnosis and solution had come not a moment too soon.

While I waited out the 3 weeks to the op, I got spiritual help from my Church, physical help from friends and was able to prepare for the worst case scenario. Dying did not scare me as I have confidence in what happens after. I made my will, tried to get all my affairs as much up to date as I could to make it easy for my relatives to handle everything if they had to.

The Friday before my op, I went for an MRI scan. I didn't have to, but I'd been asked if I would take part in a research project because of the rarity of my sarcoma. It was the least I could do, so off I went, only to discover that MRI scans are absolutely horrendous. Bearing in mind I was by this time in some discomfort anyway, it was hard to endure the added pressure of two heavy flat objects they had to lay over my abdomen. The noise is ghastly. Hammering goes on for several minutes at a time. I coped for about 40 minutes, but they let me off the final 10, which weren't strictly needed, for which I was eternally grateful.

The day of the operation came at last. I was in hospital waiting from the early hours until late afternoon, which is not conducive to your nerves. And of course nothing is allowed to pass your lips. Once you go down to theatre, you put yourself into the hands of the experts and let them do their thing.

I woke up feeling like a zombie, wires everywhere, but – surprise, surprise – I was still here.

Now I hardly ever take drugs, not even for headache. The deluge of anaesthetic for a 4-hour operation made me absolutely high for most of my time in intensive care. I swear the room kept going up and down and my head was woolly for days.

I had a high level of painkillers going in too. They give you that wonderful contraption which enables you to stick yourself with a dose whenever the pain hits. I complained it didn't work.

"That's because you have to wait a few minutes between doses," said the nurse.

I tell you that's the longest few minutes in history.

They wheeled me into a ward eventually, and into the brutal world of physios.

"Yes, you can get up. Now, come along, we need you to stand and take a couple of steps."

You tell them you can't, but you do. All you want is to lie there dying slowly. But there's no languishing in bed. You have to get up and sit up in the chair, and take walks. No mercy. But the nurses, on the other hand, are positive angels and perfectly wonderful – except for insisting you go and have a shower every day even when you'd rather stick pins in your eyes.

Speaking of which, I got used to looking like a pin cushion. At one point I was bruised from wrist to elbow. I grew to love the canulars, which meant I didn't have to endure being stuck with a needle again, though I had to learn to inject myself daily.

The surgeons visited every day, checking up, reassuring and asking if I'd opened my bowels. No. No. And no again.

This is when the complications set in. They'd had to remove a piece of bowel (along with a couple of other bits besides the kidney), and the bowel is apparently a shy, sensitive little creature and doesn't like being touched. We had to wait a few days for it to stop sulking (as one of the surgeons put it) and get itself going again.

It didn't. Instead, I started throwing up. Suffice to say that with a wound running down your tummy from groin to chest and numerous hidden stitches inside you don't want to be vomiting every time your stomach fills up with bile. Christmas went by and I stayed put. Two minor procedures later, I had a tube down my nose and a triffid of wires sprouting from my neck and was being intravenously fed and watered. I couldn't eat or drink for weeks and ended up looking like a refugee from a concentration camp, all skeleton and no flesh.

A month after the first op, after uncountable x-rays and scans, they opened me up again to fix the bowel. It had decided to protect itself by sticking itself together so that nothing could get through.
Finally, after another bout of intensive care and a week of recovery, things began to happen at the right end and I was able to start the painful process of learning to eat again. It was all over bar the shouting and I made it home at the end of six weeks, clear of cancer, skinny as a stick and ready to begin the long road to building the body up to normal.

The first time I went back to see my surgeon, I took a macabre sort of pride in learning that my sarcoma had been 13 inches long and weighed 5 kilos. It was oddly exhilarating to know the beast had been that vicious and still couldn't win.

At this writing, I'm two years clear and heading for my next six-month check. You get the scan and a week later, you go for the results. In the online sarcoma support group, we call that week scanxiety. You just can't help the niggling thought it might have come back.

Hindsight is a wonderful thing. When I looked back, I remembered having digestive problems about six months before I noticed the lumps. I'd been to my alternative practitioner, who had found an infection in my kidney and treated me for that. No sooner had that cleared up than my digestion kicked up again and this was an infection somewhere in the bowel. At the time, it didn't occur to me to relate the two. Nor could I have guessed the problems were likely caused by the sarcoma sitting up against my diaphragm.

My surgeon told me it had probably been there for a very long time, dormant and doing nothing. He said they have no idea why they turn malignant all of a sudden. Apparently it had started off as a Grade 1 (the lowest) and ended up a Grade 3 (the highest), which was why I only started to feel the effects in the last couple of months when it was growing at a hectic rate. I was getting weaker and slower, and the weekend before the operation, I was having trouble eating and couldn't keep my food down. When I saw the surgeon the morning of the op, he said the MRI scan showed it had grown perceptibly since the CT scan two months before.

It's been a long, slow road to full recovery. I was over the moon when I gained my first two pounds. Getting my strength back was a difficult process, my stomach had shrunk so much I could only eat little and often, and I had to consume fattening foods. I didn't have any complaints about that, though my portions were minute.

Last year, when I was well enough, I undertook a detox programme to get rid of all the drugs and, hopefully, the cancer cells too. I had taken a course of Essiac, imported from Canada, immediately after the operation, which has cured cancer in the past. And now I've started to work with diet as well, avoiding foods considered to be carcinogenic and eating more of the anti-cancer foods. Lots of vegetables and fruit, especially berries – blueberries in particular. Very little meat, perhaps a bit of chicken sometimes. And I now buy organic if I possibly can. I'm living on avocados, mushrooms, broccoli and sweet potato mostly. Goat's cheese rather than cow's – I stopped having milk in my tea before the op and only have a slice of lemon now. No sugar, though I indulge in chocolate now and then and the occasional scone. You can't live without a few tasty pleasures.

It just seems to me sensible to help myself as much as I can. The doctors have done their part, and continue to keep an eye on me. I don't even think of it as being in remission, though that's what it is. I just think of it as being clear and thank my stars I've been so lucky.

When I hear about the troubles of some of my fellow sufferers in the sarcoma support group, I can't help but believe I had a miraculous escape. My particular sarcoma was huge but confined to one area and it was removable all in one piece. Others have lost limbs and other parts of their anatomy which result in disfigurement or disability. They've gone through pints of chemo, blasts of radiation and still found secondaries cropping up, and we've lost a couple of members of the group each year.

So my story is one of hope. I've turned 70 and I feel I am looking forward to many more years, thanks to the efforts of my lovely surgeon and his team, and the kindness and care of the staff at the Marsden. Mr Strauss promised I could resume a normal life, and that's exactly what I've done.

I'm back writing and publishing my books, meeting friends and family, enjoying Church functions and my friends there. For most of the time I forget I ever had cancer, and it comes as a surprise when someone asks me how I'm doing.

"How am I? Well, I'm fine, of course. Why should I be anything else?"

Bio

Elizabeth Bailey is English but grew up in Africa to an artistic and unconventional family. She is a writer and her historical romances are available from Amazon, Barnes & Noble, iTunes and Kobo.

The others are as yet only on Amazon.
Full info at elizabethbailey.co.uk with direct links to purchase pages.

"As usual, there is a great woman behind every idiot."

- *John Lennon*

Kirsteen Lyons

Even in Paradise it Rains
From Martha Montour, USA

A devastating bereavement, a major life-style move, an abduction and a rape. How much can any one person take?

A little bit of background

I moved to the small village of Sittee River, Belize, in the spring of 2010. I had been traveling to Dangriga, a larger town about half way down the coast of this tiny country. At the time I began visiting, in 2008, the population of the entire country was listed at 320,000. I was coming from Denver, CO a much larger metropolis, and part of the appeal to me was this very quaint size of the country, and of course a much slower way of life.

Let me back up a bit to give a bit more insight into why a woman of only 52 would chuck her current life in the US to move to a tiny, third world country.

I worked as a Nurse from my early 20's until I retired in late 2009 after 30 plus years in the field. While I thoroughly loved being a nurse and helping other people, my current position caused me to burn out, and burn out badly! The last year of my career in Nursing found me working without lunch nearly every day; without a break and always staying late. There were many days of working incredibly short staffed and I began to fear that a patient would suffer a bad outcome from our severe lack of staffing. I weighed my options carefully and decided to retire in late 2010.

Earlier in my career however, the love of my life came into my world via my work life. I was working as a nurse at the HMO which employed me the last 23 years of my career. It was May of 1994 and the company had decided to hire a new Family Practice physician. One of the prospects traveled to our clinic all the way from a town near Montreal, CA to interview. I was walking out of a Nurse visit room when he was walking in on part of the "tour" of his visit. We shook hands, he greeted me with a hearty hello, and something passed between us. It was several months before he returned to work for us in September of the same year. Over the next few months we became good friends and ultimately we fell in love. It's not the point of this article to share much more about this, other than to lay the foundation for what became the most meaningful love relationship of my life to that point, and since.

We ultimately began a life living together in 1998; we bought a house together in 1999. Our lives were not free of conflict, but in this man I had found my soul mate. A person who truly "got me" and I got him.

In February of 2001 my beloved partner was diagnosed with Stage Four Colo-rectal cancer. There was very little hope for recovery given him by his Oncologist. We had been cohabitating for about 2.5 years and had often discussed marrying. For one reason or other, we simply had not done so. The day or so following his diagnosis he asked me to marry him and I agreed. We were married on February 17, 2001. We had a minister perform the ceremony in our house; we had a lovely fireplace which we stood in front of and both my children stood up for us. My father was able to walk me down our stairs and it was a lovely, memorable day.

My beloved husband did not respond to the chemotherapy and within a few months, it was determined that he could simply live out his life at home. He passed away on April 1, 2002 at 10:36 pm in our bed. To say that his death rocked my world would be a huge understatement! I was devastated, in spite of knowing the time was coming. With his being a physician, and my being a nurse, we both could see the signs leading up to his death. But denial is a powerful force and it still was a bit of a shock on the night he took his final breath.

I won't go further in sharing about the loss of my husband, but wanted to lay the foundation for how much I was impacted by his death. I had taken a leave of absence from my job about 4 months after his diagnosis. I reasoned that I had my entire lifetime to be a nurse, but probably only about one year to be a wife! I have never regretted my decision to be with him that last year.

When I did return to work, about 5 months after he passed away, it was very difficult. We had worked for the same company and though I returned to work in the Float Pool, which meant I was at a different location and department each day I worked, I always ran into somebody who recognized me or my name and would then reference my beloved husband. It was a mini-death for me every single day of life. I remained in our family home for five very long years. I had read that to move within the first year was to often find regret. Beyond that time frame, it became hard to leave as it was leaving all I had left of him in my memories. I did finally move to a new home I purchased in a neighboring town in 2007.

Still, I found that I was unable to shake the sense of missing something and it was a difficult period in my life. I found a bit of happiness here and there, but still struggled with mourning the loss of this precious man. In 2008 I took a Caribbean cruise which went to several ports of call. One of the destinations was Belize, where I had not yet visited. During the time I was there, I learned about their Expat program and cheaper cost of living and lack of taxes. This sounded like just what I was looking for and I vowed to check into it as soon as I returned home.

I did find out a lot about Belize and set about making a plan to visit again for a longer stay. I went to Belize in February 2009 for a week, staying in Dangriga. I loved my visit there. It was just so wonderful to find myself in this place that had no memories with my late husband, and only a clean slate in which I could create some memories of my own! I loved the tropical temperatures, the proximity of the sea and the people that I encountered. I returned home to CO after a blissful week and began almost immediately preparing for my next visit.

I returned for a week in July of 2009 and had an equally wonderful stay, again in Dangriga. When I returned home this time, I decided that when I went back to Belize that I would like to check out the village of Hopkins, about 20 miles south of Dangriga. I set about planning to go for 3 weeks in November of 2009. My plan that time was to work until the end of 2010, at which time I would retire early and then move to Belize.

Well, one of the problems I had in that job was some poor management and a declining morale. After having paid for my trip and lodging for three weeks, my manager refused to let me have the time off! I was faced with losing the thousands of dollars in travel expenses, or leaving my job early. I chose to retire one year earlier. A decision that I've come to question since, but nonetheless it's the decision that felt right to me at the time.

I did go visit Hopkins and Sittee River (a sister community a few miles from Hopkins on the Sittee River) for three weeks in November of 2009. I met several people, made some friendships and found a house that felt perfect for me on the Sittee River; actually in the jungle across the road from the river.

I went back to CO just before Thanksgiving of that year and set about putting my house on the market and making plans for the big move.

You're Going Where?

I relocated to Belize permanently on March 15, 2010. I had met the Expat (from Virginia) who was in charge of the local Humane Society in Hopkins when I visited in November 2009. I had told her that I wanted to volunteer for them when I moved there. That is exactly what I did!
At first, I was a simple volunteer who did very basic things to assist the visiting Veterinary teams from the US that traveled to the country to help with free spay/neuter clinics of the local animals. Over the next several months, it became apparent that I could utilize my RN skills and

apply them to care for the animals. As I was able to branch out and do more medical and technical jobs for the Humane Society. They offered to pay me a small salary which I gladly accepted!

It was extremely rewarding to care for the underserved animals of the country and to also help with the extreme over population of animals. I was able to help educate the children, who in turn educated their elders in how to properly treat an animal that is one's pet. I was even able to perform chemo therapy, euthanasia, IV therapy and much more.

That first summer I lived in Belize I had four part-time jobs! I was helping the Humane Society, and doing some Property Management for a friend. I also worked part time for a resort in helping with reservations and cleaning rooms and I assisted in providing games and physical exercise for a Summer Camp for the Sittee River Methodist School.

I made friends, enjoyed the sea and created a life unlike any life I'd ever lived. For an entire year, I never turned on a television set; instead I'd sit on my screened in porch and enjoy wildlife and quiet. I had long swims in the Caribbean Sea, and rode my bike everywhere. In fact, I had no other transportation for the first year I lived in Belize! I relied on friends who would take me into Dangriga twice a month when we all would pay our bills and do our shopping. It was a lovely life, and I kept pinching myself to see if I had really landed on my feet in such an exotic, foreign locale?

I had decided that rather than pay immigration every month of my life, I would apply for permanent Residency status once I'd completed my first year in the country. It is about at this juncture that the rain started to fall in Paradise.

I had gone to Belmopan, the capital of the Country in June 2011 to do some work toward my permanent residency and after a very long day arrived home about 5.00 pm to find that I'd been robbed! My house was like many others; on stilts of about 10' and so I had an entry on the ground, then interior stairs leading to a screened in porch. The door to my house was locked, but the intruder had found something to climb up the back and cut a hole in the screen. They then went downstairs to the workroom and set about using hatchet and machete to cut my door and enter my home. They stole about 300$ worth of property and cash and that was that.

The police came when summoned, but were unable to really do anything. I was able to get some help from neighboring friends who patched the screen and I was able to install several additional locks on my doors. The bloom was definitely off the rose by now, but eventually I was able to get back to the business of living and to live without constant fear of another such occurrence. The criminal was never caught, nor any belongings found or returned.

Life is What Happens When You're Busy Making Other Plans

The next year went by much as any other. I continued to work for the Humane Society and even had adopted a dog and 2 cats which kept me company out on the river. I must say that it was pretty isolated for me. My nearest neighbors were across the road about ¼ mile in distance and my house abutted to only jungle. I loved the quiet and solitude, never dreaming that it would prove to be my undoing.

In February, 2012 we had a visiting team of Veterinarian and technicians working with us at the Humane Society, so this meant about a week of days from 8:00 am until 5 pm or so of working at the clinic.
On a Tuesday morning I went outside into my van and noted that the items from the glove box were strewn about the van. I had no working locks or windows on the van, so it was obvious an intruder was rifling probably for keys to steal the van, or enter my home. I was preoccupied with getting to work and didn't really think about it a lot. That evening just at dusk, I was home from my long day and getting my supper ready when I noted that I had no gas. In Belize, people use propane tanks, mounted outside, but attached to the stove to cook.

I went outside on my veranda, and found the tank had simply been turned off. I was a bit puzzled and my big Labrador Pepe was with me at the time. We turned the tank on and back inside we went.

The following day was a Wednesday and off to the clinic I went at 8.00 am. At about 3.00 pm that day, the clinic shut down early. I was the last person to leave as I was in the process of sterilizing instruments, so I waited until they were finished and then went home. Often I took Pepe with me on clinic days, but I had left him home that day.

I had a concrete slab under my house that I could park on, then my front door was right there, and all was under the cover of the house. I recall getting home about 3:30 pm. As I walked to the door, I remember wondering why Pepe wasn't greeting me with his usual bark. I actually was in the process of speaking to Pepe as I unlocked the door.

The next thing I know, as I pushed open the door, a man was standing to the left in the corner of the door and the house. He was holding a rag in his hand and lunged at me , saying "You didn't expect to see me, Bitch". I know that I was able to croak out the word "NO!" as I tried to run out the door to safety. But he was quick and the rag in his hand was soaked in chemicals. He grabbed me with one arm around my face and pressed the rag against my mouth and nose. I was suffocating but fighting with everything I had in me! I also was becoming dizzy from the chemical fumes in the rag, and feared I'd pass out or die. I tried as hard as I possibly could to free myself from his grasp, but he was full of the Adrenalin to commit a brutal crime and the more I fought, the tighter his grip became.

I was frightened that I would suffocate to death! I was pulling his hand to try desperately to pull clean air into my nose or my mouth. He wrestled with me and threw me to the concrete floor near the bottom of the stairs leading upstairs to my house. He yelled at me to shut up! He actually said "Shut the fuck up" repeatedly and told me he'd kill me if I didn't quiet down. He pressed into my back with a sharp object and told me he had a gun. About that time I think I left my body. I mean to say that I dissociated a bit, in order to survive. It was as though I watched this playing out to me from above.

I had a friend in Belize; a fellow expat, who had been murdered several months before and her killer had never been brought to justice. As I lay there fearing I too would be murdered I "heard" her voice in my head. She told me "don't fight him and you will live; I fought him and I am dead". I heard this as clearly in my head as if she were whispering to me in my ear. I believed that the answer to my survival lay in my being as agreeable as I could be.

So, when he hoisted me to my feet and told me "You're going to show me the money" and forced me up the stairs, I let my feet propel me one step at a time. I audibly screamed when I got to the porch and saw the devastation of my beautiful home! The door was chopped into pieces and there was debris all over the porch.

He pushed me into the house and there was further destruction and damage to behold! All my belongings had been rifled through; there was food all over the counters and signs that he'd spent hours drinking and eating and smoking and gathering the items of mine to steal. He told me that the reason he didn't leave with my things was he was waiting for me to give him my money.

After the robbery the year before, I had lost all my cash as it was stored in an envelope which I kept in a locked drawer in my office. So, I had begun storing my cash by hiding it in a cookbook in the kitchen. Clearly my ruse had been effective as he had not found the money.

He threw me to my couch and took the purse I had around my neck and shoulders. I had just been paid that day and had 150.00$ in Belize money in the purse, which he took and threw the rest to the floor. I lied and said that I had no other money. He then told me "Now, I'm going to rape you". This is the hardest part for me to write about. I hate that the act of Rape causes the victim to feel shame, when it is NOT their shame to bear.

In any case, I continued to feel the presence of my friend and her admonishment to not fight; thus he took me and raped me. I realized during the assault that my lack of fight was making it difficult for him to stay engaged or interested in his assault against me. I felt intuitively that if I fought him, he'd not only enjoy the act, but he would kill me. I knew this with every fiber of my being and so I behaved accordingly.

Finally he told me that I was going to get him out of there and to freedom. He said to take him to my van and drive him out of Sittee River.
He again pressed into my back with what I believed to be a gun, as he had told me he had one. I was forced to get into the van and he lay behind me with the gun in my back. As I drove I begged him to just let me go, but he would not listen. He warned me to do nothing to signal that there was a problem as he hid below view from the road. I passed a friend of mine named Everett on the road, and I tried without words; only expression to telegraph my distress to him. It was only in my eyes, which my perpetrator could not see, as I had no rear view mirror. Sadly, Everett was unable to know that I was being held captive and so I just kept driving.

In Belize there are two Highways. I use the term Highway but really, both are only two lanes; one each direction and the only distinguishing difference making them a Highway is the ability to drive 55 mph. The junction from my home to the Southern Hwy was about 2 miles. I drove and was absolutely terrified that as we got away from people and witnesses, that he would kill me and take the van to flee from the village.

I truly didn't think any further ahead than the moment in front of me and did what I could to not lose control of myself and to stay alive. The drive to Belize City is about three hours. I had no idea where he was taking me, but as I drove on the Southern Hwy he began to talk to me. He told me that I was going to take him all the way to Belize City and that was all I knew. He was a very scary person. He was alternately threatening, telling me "I'll kill you" and then being solicitous and asking me "are you OK". It all made me feel like I might lose my mind, as I had no idea what might become of me. At one point he asked me "Do you know why I do this?" referencing the crime he was perpetrating against me. I told him no; he then told me "I have five kids and it's hard". I said nothing, though I couldn't help but think of how sad that this evil man had children dependent upon him for survival.

I was made to turn on to the Coastal Hwy which is even more of a joke in that it is completely unpaved and full of huge pot holes. My van was in terrible shape already and I feared it would break down. The route he had me take was an area of no Expats, and a very crime ridden place. I was asked, later after the attack, why didn't I jump out or try to escape.

Well, there are several good reasons for this. First of all, I had no money, no ID, no phone and only the keys to the van and myself. I had on only flip flops, shorts and a tank top. Also, I was the only non Belizean person for miles and the only female that I could see. Belize City and its surroundings are one of the highest crime areas per capita in the world! I felt that as long as I cooperated with my attacker, that I was less in danger with him, than fleeing on foot at dusk in a crime ridden area.

Eventually we arrived in Belize City. He made me drive and then he got out of the van and grabbed the backpack that had belonged to me; filled to brimming with all that he had stolen; which I had yet to learn about. He admonished me if I told anybody about what happened that he would know and he would kill me. He had been uttering these threats for four long hours and by now, this idea was deeply etched in my mind.

I drove away not knowing where I was! I had never been to Belize City and now it was dark, I was shaking with fear and adrenalin and was finally alone for the first time since I turned the key in my lock four or five hours earlier.

I drove blindly looking for the Southern Hwy and finding my way slowly back to my home in Sittee River. It was dark and suddenly the trauma rose up inside of me and I began to shake uncontrollably and to sob wildly! I felt that I would lose my grip of sanity and I quickly forced myself to rein in my terror and to drive as though my life depended on it, which in fact it probably did.

I was about 45 minutes from home, still on the Southern Hwy when my van just stopped. I tried and tried to get it to move, but it would not. I knew that it had been damaged in the drive over that rough Coastal highway with rocks pinging the undercarriage. I could not even get emergency flashers to work, nor push it out of traffic! Here I was, stuck on a totally dark, unlit stretch of 2 lane highway, stalled in the only lane leading me home!

I was panic stricken and not sure how I'd survive to get home. Within a few minutes a car stopped. I held my breath, praying that the persons stopping were not more criminals. It was an American man and woman who offered to help me. It was about 10:00 pm. They were both very young; maybe under 25. They helped me push the van to the shoulder, then had me get in the backseat and told me they'd take me to my door.
I was afraid, but felt I had to trust them as sitting on a dark, deserted highway was a much less promising choice. They drove me right to my door.

I was quite afraid to enter my home, but the man went first and unlocked my front door. I knew that my dog Pepe was in the house; the criminal had barricaded him on the first floor and I knew I had to get to him and save him from starvation or thirst. Also, the criminal had taken my cell phone from me before forcing me to drive him; he had put it in my freezer.

I entered behind the young man, and together we found Pepe who was so grateful to be freed from his enclosure. Together we all went upstairs and then the couple went on their way. I got the phone from the freezer and thankfully it still worked. I phoned a friend first, but got their voice mail. It was about 10:45 at night and most of my friends were at the bars or out doing some sort of partying. I called several people but continued to only get voice mail. I was leaving messages, and with each one a bit more hysteria was creeping into the message, but I was desperate to find somebody to help me.

My home was completely unsecured! None of the locks worked and there was a hole in the screen on the main floor where the perpetrator came in. I could not stay there another hour or longer awaiting a friend, but had no car, no money, and no way to get myself to safety.

Finally I reached a friend in Sittee River who came to me on his motorcycle and he brought with him the Sittee River Police officer. They called the Dangriga police and he stayed with me for the hour that it took for them to arrive.

I waited thinking that once the officials came, I'd be safe and I could get some help. Sadly, the officers chose to instead berate and blame me for the crime that victimized me! I was asked if I lived alone, which I replied yes to. Then I was informed that it was my own fault to be victimized in this way as I was a white woman living in a black country by myself!

They took me in the police car to Dangriga; a 30-40 minute drive from my house. I had nobody with me but the 4 officers in the car and was sitting between two in the back seat while the other two sat in the front. Two were women, two were men. All four were very mean to me and made me feel much worse than I already did. They talked about me as though I weren't there, saying things like "If it was me I'd have" and "why didn't you run away" and more inane, cruel comments. I finally had enough and said "It's fine to say what you would have done, but until you are in the situation you don't really know".

They took me to the station where I gave my statement. Finally, one of the people whom I'd called and left a voice mail for called me on my cell phone. I was assured that he would come to Dangriga and collect me. The police were rude and abrupt with me. They had taken me to the hospital prior to the police station to perform a Rape kit. But, they did a terrible job!

I had no female present with me and the female officer stood far away and left me alone. They did not comb for pubic hair; they did not take swabs to check DNA, they didn't test my clothing and they didn't protect me in any way. It was humiliating! The man doing the vaginal exam talked to another man in the room who was not even identified, about me, in front of me. For all I know, it was a janitor and not a medical person!

I finally got to leave the Police department about 3.00 am. My friend took me back to Sittee River and I got a bag and packed some clothing, got Pepe and his food dishes and then he took me to a house of a mutual friend. She greeted me with open arms, a warm embrace, tears flowing down her face.

We sat together outside under the stars and watched the sun come up as I recounted the story of my horrible night of fear.

Life After Crime

As the day began, people made their way by her home and I would get visitors throughout the day of friends who came to give me hugs and express their sorrow over my experience.
I stayed with her for about 48 hours, then the neighbor across the road who has a B&B, offered me to stay in one of her guest rooms as long as I needed. I had determined that I could never again live in my house; her offer was incredibly generous.

I did stay with her for just under two weeks and then I was able to rent a house on the beach. I loved that there was a family renting long term in the house above me and it gave me so much comfort to hear them come and go and the sounds of life above my head.

In fact, when that family moved out, I cried as now I was back to being alone. My life with constant fear had been set in motion and it continued to drain me of happiness.

One of the scariest moments I encountered multiple times a day was the act of opening the door to my home. You can imagine, the way I was assaulted, that I feared what was on the other side of the door. One of the reasons I loved that beach apartment was that it was one room; I could see the entire space when I entered and be sure nobody was lurking to get me.

I stopped going places after dark, and I carried a taser with me all the time. In fact, I slept with the taser right next to me and kept it near my hand.

Because the hospital failed to take any samples or do a proper rape kit, a friend of mine who was a nurse locally, came to me and performed an exam. She collected necessary swabs and blood for HIV testing for me. She was a true Godsend, coming to me and ensuring that things were handled properly. I was instructed to have a repeat HIV test in three months, presuming this one was going to be negative. I did test negative initially, and three months later thank God!

I had identified my attacker at the Police department in Dangriga only two days after my attack. However, he remained free and at large. I didn't know it then, but I learned that the crimes committed against Ex-pats who aren't of Belizean extraction simply carry no weight with the authorities. Thus, my attacker remains free today!

About one month after the attack, and suffering still with terrible PTSD and the weight of constant fear, I chose to go to the Mayan Center (about 10 minutes south of me) and see somebody for a Spiritual Healing. I knew a woman named Aurora who was a Spiritual healer and had made friends with many Mayan people in my time in Belize. I found the Mayan people to be so very kind, with strong family values and I had come to respect and trust them.

She spent well over an hour with me performing rituals of cleansing and she gave me a prayer to read a minimum of nine times a day for two weeks. She gave me some bitters to drink and a leaf that she had wiped away negative energy from my body. I went to the Sittee River on my way home; stood on the shore with my back to the water and threw the leaf into the water. I then watched the leaf and noted the negative energy floating away from me. This healing went a long way toward helping me recover a bit of ease. I was a very long way from healing, but didn't even realize yet just how far.

Going Home

I had been trying to return home to visit my family in Colorado, but the attack left me so shell shocked as to find leaving almost as hard to do as stay! Part of the reason it was hard to leave, was finding people who would keep my property and my dog safe in my absence. Eventually, I was able to plan a trip to return to CO for one month; from June-July 2012. I fully intended to return to life in Belize, after my time visiting, but only after getting "home" did I realize I did not ever want to go back!
It started out that I would find myself crying without any warning and without even talking about the crime itself! I cried nearly every day for the first week of my return. It was during this time that I started to allow myself to consider that maybe I didn't have to go back?

I decided after about three weeks to extend my visit by a month and thus delayed facing the return. During that time I decided that I would not return to Belize to live. I eventually figured out how to get some of my most important belongings back to CO and committed to a one year lease on an apartment in the same complex as my daughter.

I did have to go back to Belize for ten days in August of 2012 to pack up and ship what I could back home. It was important to me to say goodbye to the people who had been so good to me over the years as well. I had my house to sell, and my car as well. After the van was ruined, I purchased an SUV and hoped I could sell it.

I was so terrified to be in Belize again. For ten days I was in terror of being murdered by the man who committed the crime or one of his many family members. I mostly stayed at my apartment by myself; the taser always by my side.

I returned to Denver, CO on August 15, 2012. I spent a long time thinking that one day I'd return to Belize; maybe not to live, but surely to visit friends. Well, it's now almost June of 2016 and I've never been back.

Starting Life All Over Again

Returning to CO, I had to buy everything I once had all over again! The crime cost me so much; not least of which was lost money in the house I took a 25,000$ loss selling; the vehicle, all the belongings I couldn't get home with me. I had to buy everything one needs to start life off on their own; down to the spices in the kitchen, plates, table wear, linens and more. I furnished my apartment and began a new life. I still had some residual fear, and opening the door to the apartment was still a scary thing, though it was less scary than in Belize.

Over time I got a part time job, reconnected with friends and family and worked on making a life. I didn't realize that I was suffering until about 6 months later, when I suddenly was overwhelmed with depression, fear and a lot of anger. I was able to find a place called R.A.A.P. They are a not for profit organization that support victims of rape and violent crime. Their name stands for Rape assistance and awareness. I was given a sliding scale fee and had once a week therapy with an LCSW for five months. In the time I met with my therapist my scores for depression, anxiety and PTSD went from very high to much lower. I was able to feel quite a bit better in the process.

In the interim, my daughter moved to AZ and got married. My dear Mother became weaker over time and I was able to care for her and spend some very loving, close time together until she passed February 20, 2014.

My beloved granddaughter Emily was born April 29, 2014 and I got to be there and even cut her cord. It was one of the most precious moments of my life and prompted my own move from Denver to Phoenix, AZ in August 2014.

Life after crime has only gotten better for me. I am no longer living in a "victim" mentality. Where once watching endless episodes of crime shows and forensic programs used to fill my time, I have since stopped watching them, realizing that what we think about is what we manifest. I choose to watch things that will uplift or entertain me instead. And I read a lot!

I've taken a very long, painful journey to uncover some deep spirituality and a sense of purpose that was long missing from my life. While it may sound ridiculous to some, the horrible crime really did lead to some beautiful, positive developments in my life.

I wouldn't wish such a thing on my worst enemy, yet it has stimulated such growth in me that I could never wish away!

It really is true that from some of the darkest times in our lives, some of the most fertile growth can occur. I liken it to using manure to grow beautiful roses! Even out of something as icky and smelly as cow dung, a beautiful rose can grow.

I'm proof of this! From the ashes of a horrible crime and devastating loss, I've risen to be a more actualized, happier, spiritual person than I could ever have dreamt of being!

I'm now a writer, though my first publication has yet to occur. I am half way to being a Docent for the lovely Phoenix Art Museum, and I'm the proud mother of two incredible adult children and a lovely Granddaughter. I am loved and able to give love every day of my life.

The criminal took almost everything of any value that I ever owned; he robbed me of my sense of peace and safety and security. He hurt my physical body, he raped me and humiliated me. But, he didn't kill me!

I still live and I never take that for granted. There must be a purpose for me and I plan on doing all that I can to live the best life possible with the time I have left.

Martha Montour

www.healthbymartha.com

facebook.com/HealthbyMartha

Leanne Cooper

"Women are made to be loved, not understood."

- *Oscar Wilde*

Frances Black

"Women are foolish to pretend they are equal to men, they are far superior and always have been.

Whatever you give a woman she will make greater. If you give her your sperm, she will give you a baby.

If you give her a house, she will give you a home. If you give her groceries, she will give you a meal.

If you give her a smile, she will give you her heart. She multiplies and enlarges what is given to her.

So, if you give her any crap – be ready to receive a ton of shit!"

- *Sir William Golding 1911-1993*

Kirsteen Lyons

From a check-out queen at a supermarket
Carol Scholes

For a number of years I've worked as a checkout queen at a famous UK supermarket. I've meet a variety of people from famous singers and page three supermodel, to thatchers, farrows, jockeys, business men and women, athletes to a certain shopper that I've seen with three different wives and a multitude of kids!

These customers and my work colleagues have inspired me to write the exploits of the Checkout Queen!

When I first made my career move (if you can call it that!) was a year after the birth of my first child when the uniform was grey 'slacks' (the only way I can describe it) with a wonderful spotted blouse, which made you look like you'd got a nasty rash or you've just caught measles. In those days I would have my head stuck in the fridges, recording all stock that was going out of date, otherwise known as 'Job 14'. Whoever knows what jobs 13 and 15 were about? Anyway that's where I started and it first introduced me to some of the area's unique characters.
There were some serious bargain hunters at the time (actually it doesn't change, just the faces are different) - one I named Andy Cap and the other Ted. Ted was the quieter of the two, a rounded man with huge turn ups on his jeans, and he was often followed about by Rover, another name by yours truly, his shopping trolley. As I said they would always come in looking for a cheap deal. These two, especially Andy Cap, would grab the food and prod it into me asking if this was going to be reduced. In those days it was down to your judgement how much you reduced it by and when. Needless to say they always missed it by an average of 5 minutes!

We had a regular very old, but eccentric, wealthy lady. Although to look at her you would never have guessed it. She was affectionately known as the bag lady on the account of the number of supermarket bags she had in the back of her car, obscuring any view she might have had. It was known that 'bag lady' would go along with her stained broken nails clearing all the crumbs from the rolls and cakes displays. It was a good job that the displays were washed down each night - can you image it? Yuk! I would talk about the saliva being transferred from mouth to finger and then onto the displays but I'm sure you get the picture. For any young checkout operator 'Bag Lady' would easily bite their heads off and stick them in a stew. She liked to pack herself, putting each item into a new bag and tying it in a knot about three times. The process was painfully slow and often customers waiting would get very impatient to say the least.

She was not the only one, however, who had this habit of finger licking the crumbs out. I can remember to my horror seeing one of my child's playschool assistant's husband clearing it out. My face must have said it all as he asked me not to tell his wife!

Life was otherwise pretty tame on Job 14. My main role of recording stock was interspersed by warding off young kids who liked the feeling of pushing their finger through the meat packaging while the parent was deep in thought about the next meal. One particular angelic girl I can remember was calmly sorting out a discomfort in her nose. She looked at her finger and I can only say that it looked like she thought 'where shall I put this?' Yep, no lie, it slipped nicely into the chicken breast packaging! This was promptly removed and put into my workstation.
Andy Cap and his mate Ted did try to buy this and if I was an evil person I could have done it, but after long arguments with these two I finally got the offending package into the waste unit.

Another uniform change was now on the agenda and as I was trying for my second child I decided to opt for ordering very large blouses. There was a method to my madness as I had seen what the maternity uniform looked like - a blue wigwam! My cartoon is no joke as I'm sure my friend Teressa would agree.

However after spending a year with my head constantly frozen I was moved, even possibly _promoted_, to checkout. See, on the checkouts you are dealing with cash, and the job value is higher than Job 14, or at least it was then! So off to the checkouts I went, this is where I met my supermarket friends and the fun began!

The checkouts were set out much like a Victorian school, all facing the same way to customer services. Each was an individual unit just like those old wooden school desks. Your customer was obviously located in front of you and the customer behind you, if they really wanted to, could easily put their hand into your till and snatch the cash. Thankfully this never happened. It was also when a cheque for over £50 would have to be authorized by the section manager - could you image that now when so often just a small trolley comes over that amount?! Business cheques were only accepted at customer services and luncheon vouchers were rife.

The work was mundane but the people I worked with were fun. When I first started on checkout I would go home and try to go to sleep, only to have codes falling down like tetras. Bananas 5, kiwi 62, oranges 17 and so on. I think it was like this every night for about two weeks before my mind settled down. The job wasn't exactly hard but sometimes when you had little sleep it was hard keeping that smile going - it would have been really easy to switch off and become a complete robotic android. However we had many laughs and in those days were allowed to chat when we didn't have customers. It was rather like going to a social club and getting paid for it.

There were a number of outstanding customers, one such pair whose names I never really knew but for this I'll call them Les and Roy, after the comedians. As a kid I remember seeing a sketch called Cissie & Ada in which Les Dawson and Roy Barraclough would dress up as women, Les would always be adjusting his right boob with his wrist. Well this couple where just like them. I could see them dressing up in those frumpy old dresses. They were forever arguing about the way the shopping should be packed, the price of veg, did I think this item was nice or not - they were a class act. They would only ever go to two checkout operators so there would be great discussion as to what they got up to this time. Sometimes it would bring tears to your eyes and trying to hold it back until they had gone was a no mean feat. There is something very comical when you have a couple arguing away and playing that typical 'old married couple.'

These two like so many customers come and go, for them it was the grand opening of a new store in the next town. Those two were fun, but the next couple were just downright rude to each other. She was a very little lady about four foot and of medium stature, he was as skinny as a rake and about five foot with his grey thin hair greased over to one side. I don't think this couple ever really listened to one another but just hurled abuse. I was shocked by them, this little old woman turned round and said:
'You stupid old git you never know what we eat or how much it costs, you're bloody useless.'
After which she rushed off to get an item followed by him saying:
'You bloody old cow always moaning!'

That was one of the tamer versions of their constant bickering and abuse hurling sessions. These sessions where always very funny but there were some customers where it wasn't, in fact in this case it was heart-breaking. This customer wasn't around long although I still see her but never with her daughter. She reminded me of a vixen. Now I like foxes and like they are very beautiful but this woman wasn't. She had very thin dark eyes, a reddish complexion and crimped blondish dark brown hair. The way she would talk to her young daughter was appalling, the child was never doing anything wrong whilst she was shopping, she was always quiet and trying to help. I've seen kids help and know that some helping is not really helpful. This little girl was not one of them. I wasn't the only one to notice the mother's behaviour towards her daughter. It was cruel and my heart really went out to her. Eventually after a while one of the checkout queens decided she could no longer hold her tongue and said something. For her I guess the little girl was too close to her own daughter's age and it sparked a bigger fire. I still wonder now how that little girl is and whether we were seeing the whole story or just a part of it. In all my time at the supermarket this has to be rated the worst memory.

So then came the next change in the supermarket life. All the old tills were ripped out to be replaced with double units. We still at this point had the two conveyer belts, the bottom one still operated by the foot control pedal. It was about this time when 'runners' were introduced to help free up the line managers. For this one checkout queen would look at the rotas and organise the tea breaks and sort out any queries you had with regard to prices, replacement products etc.

As I was now working four evenings a week there were times when I would help out with this duty. It was also the time when there was a lot of thieving going on and we were all under the careful eye. We are not talking small amounts by any stretch of the imagination, there were large sums. I have no idea what these were but knew it had to be serious if the police had been called in. It usually happened on a Wednesday, my shift and the one night I would be running. It was normal practice that if the shoots weren't working you would hand your pod containing your till's takings to the runner. Even though I knew I hadn't done anything it was pretty unnerving to be looked at as if you had! Anyway myself and two friends were 'runners' and we would take it in turns to help out.

By now you may have realised that I love having fun and with one of my work colleagues I was always getting up to silly pranks. She would ask me to get, say, a cucumber and I would present her with a marrow, her face was always a picture and would go off on one telling me 'that's a marrow, not a cucumber' to which I would say 'are you sure?' and this would go on a little while.

The customer usually cottoned on to what I was up to as I always had the real item in the other hand behind my back. I can't count how many times I did this to her, it was so comical to watch her explaining the difference, the customers always seemed to enjoy this display as well and

no one ever moaned they all just fell about laughing. This prank did last for some time. Another time we worked together the roles were reversed, this time I was on the checkout. My customer had disappeared to get a forgotten item so this same colleague decided to start help with the packing. She then noticed that the customer had a couple of bags on the trolley full of food. She wasn't sure if they had come from our store or another so she told me she was going to have a look. Well the top layer was very nondescript so she dug deeper and was having a good rummage when the customer returned. The customer I don't really think saw what Teressa had been up to and just glanced at her, to which Teressa replied:
'Well she told me to!', I was gobsmacked.

The customer was looking at both of us as if to say 'what planet are you two on' So stifling our giggles we carried on, Teressa packing and me scanning. Just to make matters even more comical the customer had just brought a plant, a cactus type, and it had one single flower on it. I scanned it and Teressa then broke the section with the flower on it, we could no longer contain our giggles and starting laughing as I hid the evidence of the broken flower. It was one of those situations where the whole shopping experience for the customer was completely wrong but she seemed totally unaware of anything.

Carol Morse

Working the evening shift would be long if there were no customers, sometimes we were asked to help remove packaging from the shelves for the night team but most of the time we either sat chatting, or in my case writing stories for my son's spelling test to make it more interesting for the pair of us or there were games I made up. I could not stand being at work and having nothing to do. So the era of the games was born.

It was devised using the shopping dividers, the first was very easy, 'what animal is this?' and I would hold one end together whilst the other end snapped open and closed - a crocodile! Well there were frogs, rabbits, kangaroos and many more.

Being short I excluded myself from the next game. This was how many baskets could be piled up to take back to the front of the store. Alex was always the clear winner for this one.

Another game that we played included turning off the conveyor belt, lowering the chair while they are serving and tagging someone so the alarms go off when they left the store.

So then came the next round of changes, runners became team leaders and section managers that did run became one section manager instead of four! In my time on the tills I have managed like so many others to put my foot in it big time! After a few times of getting situations wrong you learn to shut up and try to be politically correct. To one young lad I asked if it was nice being spoilt by his grandparents. Yep you guessed it, it was his parents. I am never sure whether the parent ever heard our conversation but whenever I see them which now is very rarely they have always been very talkative and I've struck up a good rapport with them. Unfortunately, I know he had an accident and broke his ankle and later she was in a very nasty road accident. Both are ok but their shopping habits have changed like so many.

About the same time as this incident, as if I hadn't learnt my lesson, I enquired of another customer when their baby was due. To this I got a furious: *'I'm not pregnant!'*

I didn't know what to say and honestly wished the ground could swallow me up. The following week I saw this same customer and she asked me to ask the same question again, which I refused. She then announced she'd been to the doctor's and found out she was 6 months pregnant. I still see her and her daughter and we still talk about the moment I put my foot in it.

Another error that I've committed is to call out to a customer that they've left something behind and wave it in the air not considering what it is, displaying to all the other customers. I've waved condoms, hemorrhoid and thrush creams along with less offending items.

At our store we have certainly gone through many stages and different trends. When I first started working Friday nights, it would be awful with young people hanging around and causing trouble. The local youth leaders would walk around the town keeping an eye on them, there were about four adults that used to do this. Most of the kids had nowhere to go and would hang about outside the store. There still isn't much to do about the town but I suppose with the introduction of play stations and the xbox they are all now at home online playing. This one particular Friday night, I was sitting on my till serving a customer when this lad came running in. Right by my till there was a telephone. Just as he grabbed the phone - about four policemen followed in hot pursuit.

There was quite a battle with the youth shouting and spitting, the receiver was completely ripped out and was sent hurtling towards my customer. It took all four police officers to get this youth under control, hand cuffed and his feet were cuffed as well. His shoes were removed and I can remember thinking that his lovely white socks will be black before long walking on our floor and outside. Nonetheless, as staff, we had to direct all our customers around this as they were blocking the walkway and had to close checkouts down to sort the flow of customers.

What struck me as strange was not one policeman apologised for causing a commotion in our store.

Carol Morse

For a small store in a really quiet town we have had our share of excitement. This particular evening I was working, a regular customer came to my till. Now this customer I couldn't ever really work out as his dress and his social skills didn't seem to match. Was he really intelligent or not? I just couldn't fathom him out. I was serving a gentleman at the time and next there was a lady then there was the guy outlined above. The lady had put her shopping on the conveyor belt and the guy was talking to her but she seemed to look uncomfortable. With that there was a noise and when I looked in the direction, I saw the guy had dropped a gun. He made some comment about the incident and I could really see the lady looking very uncomfortable now. The guy was getting what I can only describe as too familiar with her. I finished serving the gentleman and started on the woman's shopping at which point the guy then left. We exchanged a comment about the gun and I decided to call for help.

This took some time for someone to come down to me and by this time the woman had now gone. I was then asked to go for my break and I looked out the managers regarding the incident. The Hungerford incident was only a few months old and I thought that a customer coming into the supermarket with a long gun tucked under his coat was somewhat strange. The police were called and I identified him on our cameras and they dashed off to find him as he was known to them! Case closed I thought.

The next morning I got on with my jobs, dropping the kids off at school and nursery, popping to the gym. When I finally checked my phone there were loads of missed calls and several messages from the police wanting to talk to me. I then gave a statement explaining what I had seen. The officer then informed me that they wanted to know what they were looking at before they paid him a visit and that he was known as he kept popping into the police station chatting up one of their officers. From what I was told he was let off with a warning and I was asked that should he approach my till to push security and leave the till but I never had any trouble. Just another odd incident at the store.

Yet more changes - a refit and another uniform change. This time the uniform remained the same colour but the style slightly changed. The refit brought us new tills with smaller packing ends and no more conveyor belt. The shop floor also received a little adjustment and I can remember talking to a customer / friend and making yet another joke that the big space on the shop floor was where the escalators were being put so that we were on two levels now. Well that little joke came back to me via another customer saying that our store was going to be on two levels now, how cool was that! After long discussion it turns out she'd overheard me talking and not heard all the conversation. Note to self you never know who's listening when playing about! Knights in shining armour Well speaking of which, have your words ever got muddled? One customer was really trying to help me with some large crates of beer. I inadvertently said that he was my shight in knining armour! I'm sure this is a common mistake and fortunately he and his wife did fall about laughing.

Another gentleman I met was going on his first date as I found out after I started scanning. First the flowers, then the chocolate, at which point in true style, I said something along the lines of:
'So you think your luck's in tonight then?'

Hidden under a pudding were some durex! How embarrassed was I?!
Another young man was accompanied by his work colleague, obviously a man of the world. It was this young man's first wedding anniversary and the older man was giving him some worldly advice. The conversation when along the lines of:
"You see mate, it's important to remember the wedding anniversary, never forget it and always buy a card, flowers and chocolates. That's what women want'.

Bless.

Carol Morse

Odd Behaviours - Sitting on my checkout one night completely minding my own business, finding that this particular evening was dragging, when out the corner of my eye I saw a melon flying through the air. For a moment I thought no that didn't happen. Then it happened again and the few staff that were there were now all watching. No one really seemed to know what exactly happened. Now I'm not really clear but I seem to recall that a certain customer had started throwing items around the shop. I'd heard that the customer was banned after she started launching cans of beans! I never really knew or found out why this was or what even provoked this behaviour. Why is it women that do strange things?

We had another customer that was known to like the bottle or two of wine. Once she didn't even make it to the checkouts before starting the bottle. There she was sat crossed legged in the alcohol aisle with the open bottle slurping away. Needless to say she was charged for the bottle and taken out of the store.

It's funny how the years roll on and customers come and go as their lifestyles change. There have been so many wonderful people that I've come across that have been regular customers then just vanished off the face of the world. I have sat and listened to people's days, life and troubles. Some have been very moving.

I can remember talking to one elderly man, he'd been coming to my till several times and we had started building up a rapport. He told me that he'd lost his wife about a year before. He'd said that before she died she'd spent months typing. He explained that she used to be a shorthand typist. Where she was diagnosed with an illness and what with I'm unsure but the gentleman said that she had spent about a month typing, what about at the time he didn't know. He said that it was only after her death that he'd found all these notes of how to use the washing machine, defrost the freezer and many other notes on how to look after himself. He said with tear-filled eyes she's still looking after me now. I have to say I did have a big lump in my throat and thought what a lovely couple they must have been, for her to think of him and make sure he's ok meant that he'd looked after her well.

Another customer I take my hat off to is a man of 70 years. He's seen riding around the area on his push bike. He rides miles every day - I've passed him loads of time. His bike is not a super-new one, and he wears just a padded coat if it's cold, special glasses and no helmet. This guy thinks young, acts young and believes that you have to keep using your body to keep it fit.

The self-serve tills were installed overnight giving customers the opportunity to process their own shopping. This was to be the next challenge customers faced and had to get to grips with. Now as we know I love talking to customers and also watching the silly things they do, which I will add now, we have all done! There are those that try to operate them without their glasses and come completely unstuck.

One customer that springs to mind was a lady who was complaining that the stupid machine hadn't given her any change. On looking at the screen I said that it is showing that no money had been paid. This woman launched into me saying that she had put her £10 note into there. Unfortunately I couldn't keep a straight face, smiling I informed her she had just put her money into where the coupons go. Sure enough I opened the unit up and there was her £10 note. I then posted it into the right section and out popped her change. At this point the customer had lightened up and admitted that she hadn't got her glasses, to which I really couldn't help myself and said:
"You should have gone to spec savers!"

This cracked the situation and both the woman and myself went off laughing. I have had a lot of fun in my job, met some wonderful people along the way and learnt a lot from those I have met. Many of the staff too have interesting stories to tell, where they used to work, what they used to do and how they like the simplicity of sitting on a till talking to the customers. When I moved to this area just over 18 years ago I knew no-one, now I'm fully entrenched within this community

by Carol Scholes, England

Carol Morse

Free the Bears

Mary Hutton, Australia

I am continually in awe of the courageous work in particular of women worldwide to help others in need. An abundance of individuals striving ahead for a myriad of wonderful causes. Those who care for people living below the poverty line, work tirelessly for the animals who cannot speak for themselves, and for the protection of our environment that nurtures our very survival. Intrinsically we are bound by an invisible thread; the nurturers and the peacemakers together. And we are inspired by the greatest woman out there- mother nature herself.

I had several teddy bears as a small child, as many people do. Who doesn't love a teddy bear? But to think they're being abused like they are in the wild, it's quite simply criminal.

When I first learnt about the abuse and suffering of bears in 1993 by watching a news segment and being urged by my son Simon to do something about this, I thought perhaps I would help raise awareness by getting a petition together and asking people to sign this to show they cared. I thought I would go to my local shopping centre and stand outside to get as many signatures as I could. It was a Saturday morning and I sat in the chair telling myself this was nothing to do with me, what could I do to help. I thought 'let someone else do something, it is all too hard'. I sat there for over an hour and actually getting up out of that chair was the hardest step to take but my conscious got the better of me and feeling already like a loser, I went and stood outside the shopping centre hoping to collect signatures. That was really the beginning as many people wanted to sign. But that day was the beginning of a movement for the bears. Over 500 signatures were collected during the few hours I was at the shopping centre, giving me courage and the awareness that I was a part of a network of compassionate people that cared. I knew then that we'd never turn a blind eye to the bears of our world and with the support that rallied around me, I felt confident to continue to raise awareness.

2016 celebrates the 21 years of Free the Bears Fund.

Since being registered as a charity in 1995 the Free the Bears Fund have played a vital role in the rescue, care rehabilitation of 900 bears and more than 500 bears saved from snares, syndicates and soup bowls, poachers and the illegal wildlife trade. These bears are now able to enjoy a life in world class sanctuaries built by the fund with donations from the public. Today, the bears are not only alive but they are thriving. Each one has its own personal horror story to tell how it was taken from the wild, how most saw its mother killed and suffered at the hands of its captors before it was rescued.

We are often asked by people to relate these stories and we do so with mixed feelings. We know we need to share what we have learned so that more people sit up and take action to protect bears, however we do so with a sense of guilt that somehow we have inflicted a burden on the listener. One of the greatest hurdles to overcome personally in this line of work is coping with the cruelty involved. Seeing bears traumatised, starving, blind and abused. These images never leave you. But I always urge people to understand what is happening, better the devil you know than you don't because it's that kind of knowledge that holds the power to be able to make change.

Fortunately our rescued bears do their very best to not dwell on the past but embrace every moment of their new lives.

One of the bear species I refer to are the Sloth bears in India. The bears, taken from the wild as cubs were ill-treated, starved into submission and trained as 'dancing bears' to be used as a tourist attraction. Over the course of 7 years Free the Bears, working in conjunction with partners in India, saved all the Sloth bears on the roads and placed them in sanctuaries in Bophal, Agra and Bannerghatta. Also to benefit were the Kalandar People who owned the bears. "Seed" money was given to the Kalandar when the bear was handed over to FTB. This enabled the family to begin another form of income. Also the children were able to go to school. Empowerment was given to the women who chose to use sewing machines to make garments to sell at the local market. These women gained their independence.

Some of the Kalandar bear owners are employed in the sanctuaries to take care of their bears.

After 7 years of raising awareness and fundraising and $1 million later the Kalandar Rehabilitation Program ended over three hundred years of the tradition of 'dancing bears'. There are no more of these unfortunate bears on the streets of India today.

Sun bears and Asiatic black bears are the other species of bears Free the Bears have helped. Many of these bears have been taken from shocking bear bile farms where the bile was extracted from the gall bladder to use in traditional Asian medicine causing dreadful pain to the bears. Sun and Asiatic black bears have been taken from the restaurants where their paws would be cut off while the bear was still alive to make 'bear paw soup' a traditional dish sold in SE Asia.

Our sanctuaries in Cambodia, Laos and Vietnam are home to all our rescued Sun and Asiatic black bears. We have created enclosures where some are the size of football fields. We have constructed education centres, veterinary clinics, quarantine centres and special cub facilities where very young bears can be taken care of away from the larger bears until they are able to be mixed with other juvenile bears.

2016 promises to be our most challenging year so far with major new sanctuary developments about to begin in Laos and Vietnam. Bears are being rescued all the time so more and more space is required for them to live in comfort and safety without the possibility of overcrowding. Swimming pools, climbing platforms, hammocks and multiple sources of enrichment, both mental and physical are added to every enclosure to keep the bears fully occupied. The enrichment prevents the bears from pacing and developing stereotypic behaviour. Each sanctuary will cost almost $1 million to build and staff and supply over the next few years. This sum may sound daunting but it is a small price to pay to offer these precious bears a lifeline – drawing them out of the darkness and towards a bright new day.

We employ many local personnel as keepers, in India, Cambodia, Laos and Vietnam. Our work has also taken us to Thailand and Indonesia.

Free the Bears is run from my garage at my houses which has been turned into the office, bringing overheads down. Three ladies, all part time are employed.

I myself have been involved with the fund for many years and do not take a wage. I like to think that my time spent for the bears will help the bears at no cost whatsoever. There have been many occasions where I have given various talks at schools, clubs and other places and from those donations have been given to the bears. It's a wonderful feeling to know that my time has cost the fund absolutely nothing. It's my pleasure to give as much time as I can because it creates an opportunity for someone else to come into the organisation who might be qualified in various positions. That is what gives me the greatest satisfaction. I find the rewards are significant when each bear which has been rescued comes into the sanctuary either injured or suffering trauma is completely rehabilitated and begins to enjoy life as a healthy happy bear.

We have branches in South Australia, Victoria, New South Wales, Hobart and receive support from Queensland. We also have many volunteers who help raise funds by generously giving their time and helping out whenever there is a fundraising event.

We have been most fortunate to receive wonderful support from the various governments where we build sanctuaries and care for the bears. We have been allowed to construct the sanctuaries employing local people who provide much needed labour and skills.

Donations over $2 are tax deductible in Australia thereby 100% of that donation goes to the cause.

We raise funds by Memberships, selling merchandise, people are given the chance of naming a bear, taking out a sole sponsorship of a bear, sponsoring a bear for either 6 or 12 months. People can purchase Virtual Gifts for the bears which include swimming pools, climbing platforms, treat balls, hammocks. Health checks are also available, also bowls of fruit.

We also raise funds by holding raffles, dinners, galas and take part in the many opportunities given by having community stalls.

Supporters are welcome to come to the sanctuaries to help care for the bears by volunteering their time. Accommodation is provided and advice and safety precautions are put in place. Volunteers learn a great deal about the bears during their stay and have memorable experiences to take away with them.

When you take a stand for the bears, you fight for the end. It's a big responsibility of course to start something like this because it's a long-term commitment. And I of course will continue to do that for as long as I am able because it's in my blood. Thankfully all these years on since our humble beginnings, we now have a team of people who continue to evolve the campaign. We have a Board of Management which comprises Chairperson, Vice Chairperson, Treasurer, Secretary and a Committee. Matthew Hunt is FTB's CEO and oversees the running of our SE Asia operations. There are other staff members in Cambodia, Laos and Vietnam which include the keepers and vets.

In watching that TV program, 23 years ago, I have those poor bears to thank for one of my greatest life lessons learned. They showed me the importance of helping others with no expectation of any return. That is one of the most fundamental meanings that I believe that you can take from this life. All of these years on, the suffering of those very first bears will not be in vain, but in the legacy of the 900 others that our organisation has gone on to assist. Our biggest dream from here is to see an end to the cruelly facing all bears. And I will continue to do that together with our team, one bear at a time.

To all of the women out there who thought they might be just one person, that one person can't make a difference, I'd like for you to think again. If the cause is just and you have the passion, take the first step for who knows where it will lead. Opening just one door will always unlock several more. Or 900 cage doors in the case of Free the Bears.

freethebears.org
Facebook: FreeTheBearsFund

David Bailey

Quirky Accomodation

Jess Twitchin, an British entrepreneur in Spain.

Always a confident boy, my son gleefully waves us off from his 'fila' on the first day of school. He was still not 4 but couldn't wait for this bit of independence - away from my watchful gaze.

Ruben wasn't remotely fazed by the fact we had only recently moved to Spain and he couldn't yet speak with his companions. I waited nervously for his return at the end of a long day, hoping his positive bubble wouldn't have been deflated too much.

"I've made a friend", he said full of cheer. "called Matthew".

That sounds like a very un-Spanish name, I thought, wondering if this was an imaginary friend. But no. Ru's new friend was English, and I was soon to realise that many of the school children were, alongside kids from every other European country it seemed. This made life very interesting for us. But many were English.

Perhaps we hadn't been as adventurous as we had thought when we rather spontaneously bought our villa. Still…we were very happy with our lot. The weather was glorious of course. So good we were swimming in the sea daily and playing tennis - even in the winter months. It took 2 years before we felt the need to wear full length clothes. Eventually you do acclimatise! My husband's work on the internet could be slotted around this sporty life and hikes in the nearby mountains.

The kids were soon, charmingly, singing us snippets of Spanish songs after school. Meals out, trips to the fair and regular fiestas were a joy in this beautiful country where children are welcome everywhere - even late into the night. A playful pinch of a child's dimpled cheek or knee was always accompanied by a 'que guapa!' and a lollypop.

Slowly our oh-so-English habits were slipping towards afternoon siestas,

3pm lunches - although even now our children go to bed hours before their Spanish playmates. We were slowing down, getting used to the 'mañana' attitude. We got chickens, cats and a very destructive pig and picked fruit from our own trees. There is nothing quite like a slice of a home-grown lemon in your G&T in the evening as you watch the sunset reflecting in the pool.

This life was like medicine.

Before we left the UK our existence couldn't have been more different. My husband's work - known amongst his colleagues as 'the war zone' - had drained him completely. There was nothing left of him when he got home late at night. He grunted at me, if I was still up, as he sunk into the sofa in front of the telly with a glass of wine. Meanwhile I was going slowly crazy at home. Two small children, hormone dysfunction and, apart from a friend whose humour saved me, no real help. When my husband got the chance to do consultancy work from home we knew it was time to run - to change everything.

So we ran to the Costa Blanca.

We arrived in an orange VW camper van crammed with only our most prized possessions. We didn't need things. We needed fresh air and fun and freedom. The Type 2 van, rarely seen in Spain, created quite an excitement which made us feel like film stars as we posed for photos with her and returned waves along the way. Unfortunately our moment of fame was fairly short-lived as with her first hiccup we realised that we couldn't get the parts for her locally and she wasn't too happy with the hilly terrain either, so it was decided she must be sent home alone, forlornly, for sale.

Although it felt great to be captains of our own ship again, I quickly realised my naivety in thinking that we were pioneers, and as the years passed it did start to dawn on me that a Spanish holiday town was not the long term future I had dreamed of for me and the children.

We learnt Spanish and integrated as best we could - and we made lovely friends (mainly with other foreigners) and had a wonderful life. But....yes, there was sadly a But....as a hard-core traveller there was something missing for me. I had lived a nomadic life for my entire 20s and, although I felt very at home abroad, I had never imaged living as an 'ex-pat'. In this life people come and go, jobs are seasonal and, despite lots of friendly interaction with the local Spanish community, I was never going to belong.

Living abroad can be challenging. Much as I love this country, the tangle of red tape here is frustrating. The language was like an onion - there was always another layer. I was doing fairly well, and even taking classes in that elephant that loomed in the room - Valenciano - the locally spoken language which the children mostly studied in at school. But as we lived, the 4 of us, as an English family at home I was unlikely to ever fully master it. I made many a linguistic error on my way, and even had a Spanish friend stop being one for reasons I never did find out. A terrible social blunder no doubt. The only way to become fluent would be to have a torrid affair with the pool man or be put in prison. But that seemed a bit drastic.

The children were multi-lingual and happy-go-lucky - despite almost suffocating underneath an endless pile of homework. They were still very English of course, with English friends and sometimes I cringed when they wouldn't swop to Spanish when in a mixed group. It wasn't quite how I had imagined it.

My husband wasn't preoccupied with any of this. He loved the fantastic cycling, was attempted kite-surfing, and had a mixed nationality group of sporty friends, who spoke English with him. His lifestyle had greatly improved - as had his personality and his drink habit.

But I was the one going to school meetings and trying to blend in at the kid's parties. I was neither clinging on to my Englishness, nor slotting in like a local. I was drifting somewhere in between. I began to think this wasn't quite my spot. Spain yes, but somewhere else. I had to convince the family to move again!

In the meantime the kids were getting older. It was time for me to go back to work. But in Spain, in the middle of 'la crisis', with error-littered Spanish and an aversion to cleaning holiday villas (well, my own home even)....I would need to use my imagination.

On our next holiday, on the way to Granada, we broke the journey at a little place with a cave room and a tipi. Wow! So much more interesting than an ordinary hotel stay. We were hooked and vowed to stay in unique places everywhere we went. This was the inspiration I needed. It was quickly decided that I would put together a directory of such places from all around the world to help people like us go on that type of holiday. Castles, boats, lighthouses, glamping, train carriages, themed hotels. As soon as I started to do some research I realised that there was an endless list of amazing places to add to my new directory. So **QuirkyAccom.com** was born and I was kept busy from then on.

Now the site, 4 years later, receives over a million visitors a year and has more than 1200 properties to share with our growing number of fans. Living abroad has pushed me to be entrepreneurial and I am really proud of what I have achieved.

With **QuirkyAccom**.com set up, I started thinking about the move. Trawling the internet and driving around the orange groves and rice paddies led me to a larger town close to Valencia. This part of the coast further North attracts less overseas tourists and I felt it was more like the Spain I had been looking for. I found a school that would focus my boy's big personality and help both of him and my daughter feel at least 'Spanglish'. It was still in a place close to the sea and mountains that we all loved so much, but without the holiday feel. We rented a house and relocated.

I immediately felt we were welcomed and we all spoke better Spanish that year from the increased attention we received. It wasn't a totally smooth ride, and I felt responsible for anything that did go wrong as I had been the driving force behind our move, but 2 years in and this is home. I've found my place and may never leave it.

Jess was born and grew up in Surrey, and despite spending all her 20s travelling solo around the world, she married Dom who she had been to school with. They have 2 children Ruben and Asha. The family enjoy various sports, and travel whenever they can - helped by the fact that Jess has created an unusual accommodation directory called **QuirkyAccom.com** that features unique places, that she really ought to visit, all around the world.

Mandy Broughton

"Being a woman is a terribly difficult task, since it consists principally in dealing with men."

- Joseph Conrad

Sleeps with fishes
Teija Devere, Finland

facebook.com/teija.devere
twitter.com/TeijaDee
teijadee.wordpress.com

Teija DeVere is a 30 - year old Finnish Copywriter living in Maine, USA. Her two burning passions are dressage riding and creative writing. She is terrible at cooking, small talk and dealing with conflict. Her talent lies in working with animals, learning from mistakes and seeing the goodness in people.

One of the longest nights of my life was spent on an air mattress in Fallbrook, California. That night I didn't catch a second of decent, deep sleep. As I lay on my air mattress, in an apartment built on the second floor of an old garage building, I listened to a couple of rats who were having a slumber party in between the ceiling and walls, a thought kept entering my mind; we might just die tomorrow. We are leaving California to drive across America in an already broken pickup truck. With our pickup truck we call "Gertrude", we will be pulling a trailer which resembles more of a meth lab than an old KenCraft camper. We bought this suspicious camper from an even more suspicious man living on the border of south San Diego. The suspicious man lives in an old camper at a construction yard. The suspicious man also began texting us for a week and a half at this point, asking if we could send pictures of his previous camper once we arrive at our destination on the east coast. Wisely I think, we have not replied to his requests.

All of our earthly possessions and couple old Finnish wood chairs are now resting in an organized mess inside the camper. After packing and re-packing everything three times using some serious Tetris skills, all of our belongings are finally tucked in Gertrude's traveling meth lab. After my sleepless night and all our re-packing complete, we take off with our wobbly load hoping to leave California behind us before the sun sets. It is not long before we realize that with her heavy load, Gertrude is not able to travel faster than 40 miles per hour. Our little fortune weighs more than it's worth. We also soon find that if we try to drive faster, one or all of three things will happen; First, Everything starts to shake like we're in a middle of an earth quake, Second, I am more and more sure we're all going to die, and Third, Gertrude will over heat under the California sun with her heavy load. I may have neglected to mention that we do have some things of value traveling with us; one dog, two bunnies and about twenty Koi fish. It would be great if they would stay alive on this nerve wrecking trip as well.

I realize we have something going for us on this unorganized trip of ours. It is the fact that, at this point, we are close to being some level of professionals when it comes to moving. We drove to the west coast-in the same old pickup and survived. However thinking back, that trip didn't really go as planned either. One night somewhere in some very dark Nebraska countryside, our trailer got stuck in a muddy ditch with a ten meter fall. It was 4 AM and pouring rain. If I've learned anything about moving it is the following fact; if it rains and it's the middle of the night, then something's about to break. And so I should not have been surprised when it happened this time as well, while driving on a pitch dark highway in northern Texas. While trying to find an exit sign in the pouring rain, the road looks more like an ocean than concrete pavement. People are still driving right on my bumper, annoyed by my snail like speed. When I finally find an exit, something in Gertrude crashes and it takes all my arm strength to move the wheel. I somehow am able to turn on my emergency lights and as they are blinking wildly, I somehow pull into a gas station parking lot. That is where Gertrude decides to take a three day nap.

I've always wanted to visit Texas. Thanks to Gertrude, this wish has finally come true. Our first sweaty and buggy night is spent on a towing bed, in the back yard of a car repair shop. In the morning we learn that the closest hotel is a couple miles away from the shop and the little town we pulled into during the night in the rain has no cab service. Some friendly Texans promised to give us a ride and were somewhat amused as we pulled one rabbit after another out of our broken truck. As a final touch, out next comes a care free and very energetic pit bull who sits next to the bunny cage wildly excited about this new, cool adventure ahead. The friendly Texans drive our herd to a small hotel where we count our last pennies and wait for Gertrude to receive the TLC she needs for the next two days.

My panic attacks lessened as one incident after another occurred on our trip. It began about halfway through our journey, nervous gagging changed into nervous giggling. We spend a night under a tornado warning in Kansas. We were on the verge of sleeping when we were awoken by the wind blowing out a window on our camper/meth lab. At this point, this incident only receives a slight lifting of shoulders and we leave further inspection of any damage for the morning ahead. Without too much hesitation I can say that we started to have a bit of fun on this ridiculous road trip.

Our trip would not be complete until we had crossed through about ten more states, gotten a flat tire in Michigan, lived through an overheated engine in Vermont's Green Mountains and, of course, maxed out a couple of credit cards. At some point we counted how much money we spent on gasoline between the state of California and the state of Maine. I don't remember the amount but I do remember how nauseous it made me. The thousands of miles between the rats playing on the ceiling to my in-laws guest bedroom in Maine were so full of excitement that I didn't want to sit in a car for more than couple hours at a time for the next half a year. It has now been a year and a half since our amateur RV trip and I can now laugh out loud about it. For some reason I wish I had pictures of that unlucky garage in Texas and of the gas station where I thought our lives were over. We may always want to forget the bad stuff that happened to us and I might be a bit crazy but for me the bad stuff has now changed into good memories and moments that I can be proud of. Yes, we drove 3000 miles in an old rusty pickup truck. Yes, most of the way we drove 40 miles an hour looking like drug dealers with the worst disguise ever. It didn't help that the dozen Koi fishes died somewhere in New Mexico making the camper smell like we were travelling with dead bodies. No, believe it or not, not one time did the police pull us over.

So what is the meaning of this fish smelling story of mine? Maybe, that when you think you are living the worst time of your life, you are actually in the middle of a journey you later wish you would have taken pictures of. Maybe all of life's misfortunes have a meaning - and if not a meaning, a lesson. My slightly stupid mind has learned more from the bad times in my life than the good ones. Not one mistake has happened for no reason. Even with that being said, I have decided to travel my next thousand miles without Gertrude or a fish smelling meth lab.

> "Why are women... so much more interesting to men than men are to women?"
>
> - Virginia Woolf

Daryl Tipping

"If women ran the world we wouldn't have wars, just intense negotiations every 28 days."

- *Robin Williams*

A disappeared daughter

Catherine Broughton, English in France.

turquoisemoon.co.uk

When we looked at Debbie, just turned fifteen, we were proud. Tall and a bit on the thin side, with an abundance of auburn hair that she kept in a plait down her back, she was as pretty as a picture, cheerful, funny, clever, energetic, loving and sensible.

Well, we thought she was sensible. There was nothing about her – nothing – to give us an indication as to which way she was going. She was slightly unimaginative in the clothes she wore, she showed no interest in cigarettes, clubs, boys. She watched kids' programmes on the TV and rarely listened to popular music. She has lots of friends. In fact, if anything, we considered her a bit immature for her age.

So when, one summer's day, she disappeared with a 35 year-old criminal who had just got out of prison, we were flabbergasted. Utterly, completely and totally flabbergasted. It felt like being whacked over the head with something heavy. The shock and disbelief was massive. We just couldn't get our heads around it.

Several excruciating weeks went by. My husband, Euan, was convinced the man in question had taken her against her will. To the local people we seemed to be very wealthy. This was rural France where nothing had changed for many years. Was it possible this horrible man had grabbed her and was going to hold her to ransom?

Like the police, who got involved of course, my gut feeling was that she had willingly run off. Based on nothing other than the instinct of a mother, I felt she was just being excruciatingly naughty. With the help of a policewoman who seemed to be no older than Debbie, I trawled through her things in her bedroom. Dolls, teddies, books, crayons, some music, clothes, magazines, a tiny bit of make up, postcards of puppies and kittens. What had gone wrong and why?

Debbie came back to us, her tail between her legs, some four weeks later. Euan and I had torn the village apart trying to find her, had put up posters and contacted everybody and everything we could think of. I am a very positive person and remained calm and collected, safe in the knowledge that everything would be fine in the end, but poor Euan developed Meniere's, a stress-related disease, from which he has never recovered.

I wonder whether we should have thoroughly punished her? And how could we punish her? Something had gone wrong for which we, her parents, were ultimately responsible. Neither of us felt that punishing her (no pocket money? No new clothes? We couldn't ground her because there was nowhere to go anyway) – would these things have solved the issue? I think not.

So we carried on as normal. She went to school, we all went skiing, I tried to encourage her to invite female friends round … and after the initial awkward and hurt first week, she seemed fine.

But barely six months later, a few weeks after her sixteenth birthday, she met an Algerian gentleman by the name of Hussein. He was in his late twenties and worked as a bouncer in a night club. By this time Debbie had changed quite a lot. She had developed a figure, wore a bit of make-up, and – contrary to the way she was not even a year earlier – she seemed considerably older than her years.

At first Hussein seemed to be all right. He was clean and correct and took great care with everything. Punctual, polite, respectful, he could also be very funny and, although we were not keen, we accepted him warmly in to our household and tried to make Debbie feel that it was fine.

Perhaps we tried too hard? In no time Debbie was pregnant. Upset that she should have taken this path, I did my best to look on the bright side. I couldn't see a bright side, but felt that surely there was one somewhere …

Debbie shared a flat with Hussein then, and a bit at a time Euan and I were cut out of her life. Hussein was slightly aggressive when we went round, Debbie was studying the Qu'ran, she had to keep her arms and legs covered and by the time the baby was born – a little girl –we were not allowed round at all.

Debbie disappeared for four years.

We had no idea where she was and we both refused to voice the fear that Hussein had taken her to Algeria. Every day I thought I could see her – there, in that car! Or there! Look! On that bus! This time Euan took a leaf from my book and remained calm. We both knew that Debbie was intelligent and competent. If she ran in to trouble, if she was unhappy or felt threatened, she would find a way out. She was wily and sharp, tri-lingual and – God knows! – good at deceit. If she needed to escape a bad situation, she would. So we waited.

And that is precisely what happened. Precisely that. Four years later, now with a second baby, she escaped, all but running for her life.

And that silver lining I was looking for? I found it. That is something I always say to others when things appear to have gone badly wrong – there is almost always a good outcome, even if it seems impossible at the time. Debbie and her two babies, now aged 3 and one year, returned to us. We had to hide her for a while and, because Hussein was determined to take the children back, Debbie had to change her identity. And we, as initially unwilling grandparents, came to love and adore those babies and in no time filled a positive and wholesome gap in their little lives. We all moved back to England. Debbie is my best friend. We see each other several times a week and her children are very close to us. She took the scenic route … but now I couldn't ask for better.

Catherine Broughton has written a book about her life in France and Debbie's exploits. "A Call from France" on Amazon, kindle or paperback. More about Catherine Broughton and her work on: turquoisemoon.co.uk

David Bailey

Giving birth in a third-world country

Cheryl Rowland-Nunez, Belize, Central America.

I had a few different options for where to have my baby. I knew I did NOT want to have my baby in a Belize public hospital as I had heard stories about the treatment of birthing mothers and I did not want to be in that situation. I wanted to have my baby in a safe and caring way. I wanted to have control over what happened to me during the labour and I did not think a public hospital here in Belize would give me the experience I was looking for. My three options were: 1. Travel back to Canada to have a hospital or home birth. 2. Have the baby at a private hospital in Belize City. 3. Have a home birth with a midwife I had found by an online search. We decided not to take a chance with going to Canada if Luckie had problems getting his visa. I did not want to get stuck last minute making a plan B. I had been getting my prenatal care at the private hospital in Belize City which was a very good facility but still a hospital with policies and procedures that did not really allow me to have everything I wanted. So we chose to go with the midwife. I really wanted to have a water birth and we had met with the midwife and really liked her. She is a woman who worked as a midwife for many years in Canada and the US, highly qualified and experienced with more than 1500 births. She and her husband moved to Belize to retire but she continued to catch babies calling herself "midwife without borders" travelling all over the world delivering babies. I had contacted her and she was available at the time of my due date.

Luckie was a little unsure about what I was talking about but after meeting with the midwife he was feeling much better about the birth I wanted and confident in our midwife. Men in Belize often do not want to attend the birth or are not allowed to do so and so you can imagine what he was thinking about my birth plan. I insisted that he be there even though he was thinking it might be a better idea for him to stay back and work as much as possible.

We decided instead of having the midwife come to Hopkins where my back up hospital would have been Dangriga (I did not want this, I do not like the care I have seen at the hospital there) we decided to go to her. I would travel up to Corozal two weeks before my due date and wait. We happened to have some friends who live there also and they kindly offered us their home while they would take a vacation to Mexico.

I travelled up to Corozal by plane (small local Cessna) on Jan 4th. Shortly after arriving things got very uncomfortable for me. Every time I would walk I would experience fairly uncomfortable Braxton Hicks contractions and I was done with the swelling and just being big and awkward. I had a feeling like I should just take it easy and not move around too much until my Mom and sister arrived on the 7th. Luckie stayed back in Hopkins to work and we agreed he would come up on the 14th unless I called him up earlier. I was due on the 18th. My Dad was also scheduled to arrive on the 12th. So anyway I parked my pregnant butt in the hammock and didn't leave the house until the 7th. I enjoyed those few days as much as possible knowing that these may be the last days I would spend alone for a long long time.

The 7th finally arrived and I was quite excited to see my Mom and sister. They arrived that evening around 7pm and we agreed to meet for dinner. I walked down and met them at a restaurant near the apartment they had rented. After dinner my sister walked back with me as she was going to stay with me at the house.

I woke up at 12:30am to use the washroom and felt wetness as soon as I got up. It was like I peed myself but different, I had no control of it and almost immediately realized my water was breaking. I used the washroom and then woke my sister. We called the midwife and started to prepare things for labour to start which it did about 1:00am. I called Luckie and told him to come. It was a 5 hour drive for him and he had not really arranged anything or anyone to help him get to Corozal yet so he had to call his friend out of bed and they started the drive.

The midwife came and we headed over to the apartment to set up there. When we got there we discovered there was no hot water and no gas in the tank to heat up water on the stove so we had to go back to the house I was staying at. My labour seemed to progress fairly quickly and I was having contractions 5 minutes apart almost right away. A few hours in and I was worried Luckie wouldn't make it. I cried a little about this and that was the only time I cried. I desperately wanted him to be there when his daughter was born. We were texting each other the whole time. I was updating him on my condition and progress and he was updating me on his location. He arrived around 6am and things got pretty intense after he arrived. I got into the pool and it was amazing how the warm water cut my pain in half. My team was awesome. The midwife checked on me every so often to see how things were progressing and the baby's heartbeat. My sister is a doula and she played the most active role in clocking my contractions and offering guidance and assistance. Both my mom and my sister were very encouraging and supportive. Luckie was so calm and he was my rock which was a bit surprising. I thought he would be more tense and nervous but he seemed so calm and was there for me doing just what I needed.

When the baby started to crown Luckie got into the tub with me. Previously the midwife had told Luckie he could catch the baby if he wanted to. When it came time he was sitting behind me and wasn't sure he could get around me in time so I just spun around in the water. I really wanted him to catch our baby!

I guess one of my biggest fears was to tear so I worked really hard to not push too hard and ease the baby out as slow as I could. Resisting the urge to push her right out was the hardest part of the whole thing. I also remember feeling so exhausted at this point. I was getting very little rest between contractions.

Khaya was born into the water and Luckie's waiting hands at 8:30 am. She was removed from the water and given to me. It took her about a minute to take her first breath. She seemed so calm that I wasn't worried. She just looked at me and I looked at her, finally we meet!

I was transferred to the bed and we waited for the placenta. The cord was cut by Luckie once Khaya was breathing and the cord was no longer pulsating, there was no rush to cut the cord. Khaya stayed on my chest, skin to skin, and we waited for her to find and latch on to my breast by herself. It is called the breast crawl an it it pretty amazing! A newborn has the ability to crawl up a mothers chest and root around, using smell and touch to find the nipple and latch on all without assistance. It took Khaya about an hour to do. Allowing a baby to do this sets them up for good latch and breastfeeding success.
Luckie's experience of the birth was very positive and he felt an immediate bond with Khaya. He had to go back to Hopkins shortly after but he did not want to leave us.

After my experience I could not imagine giving birth any other way and recommend a home birth to anyone with a healthy and normal pregnancy.

I felt empowered and satisfied with how everything went. The labour and delivery progressed at my pace, no one rushing me, no one slowing me down, no one cutting me or poking or prodding me. I could walk or lie down or sit or do whatever felt right at the time without being attached to a bunch of machines restricting my movements. Instead of listening to a doctor tell me what was happening to my body I had the peace to be able to listen to my body tell me what was happening. It was not a medical emergency; it was a natural process that I was designed to do. It was hard and it was exhausting but it was awesome!

Bio: Cheryl is Canadian and lives in Belize with her Belizean husband, Luckie. Together they run Happy Go Luckie Tours in Hopkins Village, in the Stan Creek area of Belize.

Brian Thornton

A heartwarming appeal from a dog-lover in Ukraine.

From Tatyana Mizun, Ukraine

youcaring.com

(Original wording left – it is charming and the editor feels it may help the cause.)

I am Tatyana, and my mother Antonina who decided to rescue stray dogs. The local authorities have no interest in rescuing these helpless dogs. They get kicked around, starve to death, and often get beaten to death. Their lifes are not safe. Obviously there is no interest in finding a human solution, working with animal organizations, neutering and finally adopting these dogs. Therefore we made the decision on construction of a civilized shelter for stray dogs.

We operate out of our home using our private funds. We have 34 dogs to take care of. We try to re-home the dogs. The adoption donations we receive and any donations and funds are used to obtain additional dogs as well as to feed, shelter and give medical treatments the ones we have. All of this is at our personal expense. The dogs have dog houses to live in. We will take in as many stray dogs as we can. Right now more than 10 dogs are not sterilized. Only serious spay and neutering programs will solve the problem of dog-overpopulation.

Our plan to start with the construction of the shelter in autumn. The shelter will be build in our yard. For construction we found builders who made the estimate for 7500 dollars. This will be only possible with your understanding and kindness.

God will never forget your good acts, and will send you pleasure and health!

As interest of people construction of our new shelter grows, we can't but simply share that is already made and prepared. The shelter will be is under construction thanks to your help and support, therefore our purpose to tell and show you about the construction plan. Construction of a shelter was planned in 2014 in the summer, we began fund raising in the winter, but passed already a lot of time, and we can't collect a necessary bag. Now construction is appointed to spring of 2016 if funds are collected.

During the last days we prepared updating on the collector of donations, all councils which experts of veterinary science and civil engineering firms shared were collected, and also we listened to recommendations of other shelters in Kharkov where we visited on a visit. We prepared the final model of a shelter, defined what cages of type will contain dogs (see a photo) what will be ventilation and system of heating. Besides sellers promise a discount for construction material, in view of that our project isn't commercial.

At the moment, we received $470. Other bag still is in bank in Holland which in some days will come to Ukraine. $70 paid treatment of a cat "Smoke". $200 paid for production of technical documentation on permissions of construction of a shelter. We provide checks about payment
We think that it becomes clear to you that wishing to equip completely a shelter, all of us still are in your financial support in great need.

Carol Morse

"Man does not control his own fate. The women in his life do that for him."

- Groucho Marx

Brian Thornton

Kipling County Carriage Driving

A voluntary organization for the disabled, England.

From Annette Thornburn, Sussex.

Many of the volunteers that work here are women. We are people who wish to help disadvantaged people, and who love horses.

Kipling County Carriage driving benefits a group of people with disabilities, and it functions under the supervision of the RDA (Riding for the Disabled Association). It originated in Burwash where Rudyard Kipling spent many years - hence the name.

Like any association, we have a committee and a small group of volunteers, some qualified to assist with the disabled and some not. We fill all sorts of roles from committee members, to people who help with the horses, and companion carriage drivers called "companion whips".

The whip's role is to sit next to the driver with an extra pair of reins, and this is an important safety precaution. Of course we need people to hold the horses while wheelchairs are being loaded or disabled drivers are being helped on to the carriage.

Kipling owns two horses who are kept at a yard at Burwash, and cared for by a volunteer. Both horses are senior and are due to retire soon. Two of our volunteers bring their own horses to help out.

We meet, weather permitting, in a couple of nearby fields. Before each session the field is set up with a series of obstacles - numbered cones or barrels - which the driver must pass through. We also have an area where they can practice a dressage sequence.

Our drivers have a variety of disabilities. Some will progress to driving independently, and others will always need extra assistance. Many are ambitious and attend various shows throughout the year, or they com-

pete with other RDA riders. This, in turn, involves transport, but it is important that our members enjoy the challenge of competing.
Whatever the problem we always do our utmost to accommodate members and often get excellent results.

We have wonderful results with this charity and we change the lives of many disabled people for the better.

However money is the constant problem, our overheads are enormous and the horses' needs continuous. There are trips to the vet, shoeing, rental of the fields, and so on. In order to cope we have fairly regular fundraising activities, for example musical evenings, quiz nights, and the Christmas fair – and several other events.

As volunteers we get enormous pleasure from the group and we only have to see the smiles from everyone involved to feel it is so worthwhile. More volunteers welcome!

Kiplingrda.org.uk

Mandy Broughton

The Barrel Boutique

Jane Griffin

Bio: I'm Jane Griffin, a happily married, British born mother, living in the Languedoc Roussillon Region in the South of France. In 2006, I gave up a successful career in the UK and crossed the English Channel to France on a 70 foot long Dutch Sailing Klipper. Since then I've travelled 11,000 kms on the barge, rescued a dog, managed a ski hotel in the French Alps, become a mother, renovated an 18th Century village house and started my own business.

About the business:

While we travelled Europe's canals and rivers from 2006 to 2013, I maintained the many different types of wood on an historic Dutch sailing barge. This involved hours of sanding and varnishing and many buckets of varnish. During that time my enjoyment of woodworking grew and developed into a passion. I loved working on the lea boards, window frames, doors, mast and booms, letting the beauty of the wood grain shine through.

In 2013, my husband and I began to renovate an 18th Century village house and ancient stable building. I didn't need to look very far for decorative inspiration for our new home. The Languedoc Roussillon Region is the largest wine making region in France and I realised that I had access to used French Oak Barrels. Soon I had made a barrel feature for the breakfast bar in the kitchen, a barrel based window seat which doubles as a wine bottle store, a barrel bath side, a barrel medicine cabinet....the list goes on and on. To be honest, I became a bit barrel obsessed and had to stop!!

The unblemished French oak used in my locally sourced wine barrels is truly stunning. It was whilst creating these initial decorative pieces from the aged, curved, wine stained oak that I realised its potential for a new business venture.

At around the same time, my daughter started nursery school here in the village. Once she began to spend the mornings in school I realised I needed to work again to occupy my time and challenge my mind. My passion for woodwork and recycling needed fuelling and so, after many discussions and a fair bit of research, 'The Barrel Boutique' was born in September 2014.

I found that setting up a small business in France was fairly straightforward. I registered online as an Auto Entrepreneur. I came up with a name, bought some new tools, printed off some business cards, sourced a few barrels, built a small workshop within our stable building and began to create! Within a month I had crafted enough stock to have a small stand at a local artisan market and within a couple of hours I'd had my first sale. That market spurred me on to make some more unique products and expand my business. Following this I had stalls at Christmas markets and created my website. A friend in the UK commissioned me to make a bespoke wine rack for his home. Then I received a large order for sharing platters for a local hotel. I sell through a local gift shop, have stock in various wine growers outlets in the region and export regularly to the UK. The Barrel Boutique had really taken off!

Initially I bought my barrels from an intermediary (he had sourced them from a wine grower directly and therefore wanted his cut!) and they were quite expensive. Within six months I was approached by a local wine grower who needed to purge some of her older barrels and with that the mutually beneficial working relationship with a local Chateau began. Her barrels are of a very high quality so the oak I'm now working with is exquisite! I feel very lucky to have this relationship.

As I'm sure you already know, wine barrels are, well, simply put, er..... barrel shaped, rounded, curved, red wine stained, and each one is absolutely unique. Once taken apart, each barrel stave is a different width and as they dry out, they don't always stay curved to the same angle, which in turn means that they are sometimes really difficult to work with. Each piece I recycle is challenging in a different way. Sometimes, the inner red wine stain is covered in a glistening, thick layer of sugars and residue which needs to be carefully removed. Some days I am covered from head to toe in a pink dust! On other barrels there are tiny stones embedded into the outer part of the barrel stave, illustrating clearly how the barrel has been rolled in the wine storage cave or while being transported. Their history is rich, unique, and of course, the barrels display their scars.

Once I've created a piece, it is carefully sanded, polished and then varnished or oiled to an extremely high standard. The absolute best part of my work is seeing the delight on a customer's face as he or she discovers, touches, feels and envisages the piece in use in their home. It gives me so much pleasure to know that my creations are being enjoyed and used all across Europe. Even after a long tiring day in the workshop, when my shoulders and arms are achingly sore, and I'm covered from head to toe in sawdust, I can safely say that I love my work!

My website is www.thebarrelboutique.com

MT

Not in a million years
By Anabel Lamshire, South Africa

For security reasons this author has used a false name.

Not in a million years would I have thought it. Never. In fact it took me so long to take it on board that I said nothing, did nothing, till it was way too late.

Fin and I met at a dance. Nothing remarkable. Just a charity fund-raiser of some sort, put on by the firm that I worked for. He was invited by somebody who knew somebody … and that is how we met. I was twenty-eight and he was thirty.

I am not going to pretend it was love at first sight because it wasn't. I liked him well enough, and he like me, we carried on seeing each other off and on, then it became more regular, then it became very regular and then we were engaged, and then we were married.
From the date we met to the date we got married was a space of almost two years. Long enough.

We were happy. I continued with my job as a PA in the same firm, and Fin carried on his job as an insurance broker. I never questioned his work – there was no need to. We bought a modest house on the outskirt of Pretoria, with a huge mortgage, re-decorated, and talked about one day having a baby.

There was nothing, absolutely nothing, to indicate to me that he was anything other than what he said he was. I met his family – quite large – and he met mine. We bought each other presents on birthdays and at Christmas, we went on a couple of holidays – once to the Cape Town and once to the Kruger. I didn't wonder how we afforded it because we were frugal. We didn't penny-pinch but we rarely splashed out either. Life was good. Soon I found that I was pregnant. We were both delighted.

I suppose the first warning signs were then. You can't blame me for not seeing them. It was nothing obvious.

We had got a new car the previous year. Not brand new, a year old, and a BMW. Fin paid cash for it. He said he had been saving a long time for it. It crossed my mind at the time that I had no idea he'd got so much in savings – but I thought no more of it.

Fin was very much the wearer of the pants in our household. He made the decisions, had sorted out the house and the mortgage, sorted our holidays, always paid when we went out for a meal, was generous with gifts to me and his family. Nothing over-the-top, but generous. Like with the BMW, it crossed my mind, but then I forgot about it.

When we found that Suzy was on the way he called in decorators the moment we knew it was a girl. The second bedroom had to be totally re-decorated with fairies and flowers. I told him it wasn't necessary. In fact I told him it was all too much of a rush, that I'd prefer to take my time. But he was so excited, I let him get on with it.

I got slightly irritated when he bought cradle, buggy, kiddy furniture without consulting me. I mean, most mums like to choose, don't they? He kept saying that nothing was too much for his girl and if I tried to tell him he was being overpowering he'd get hurt and ask which item I didn't like … he just couldn't see that he was cutting me out.

Suzy was born a month early. I phoned Fin on his mobile and told him to get to the hospital because my waters had gone and I'd called an ambulance. I just couldn't believe it when he said he'd got a big meeting on, something crucial, and that he'd get there as soon as he could.
I'd been in labour several hours, and was already in the delivery room just moments away from the birth when he turned up. I forgave him instantly for he was red from rushing, sweaty, very flustered. And Suzy was beautiful.

Fin was often away overnight. This was nothing new because his job had taken him away to other parts of the country for two or three days at a time ever since we first met. I have to confess that I didn't mind at all when he had to stay away. He was quite a full-on guy and it gave me a respite, even though I loved him.

So far all I had to make me raise an eyebrow, so to speak, was the fact that he never seemed too short of money. But I was glad of it, as any wife would be. I knew what his income was, which was no more than mine – not a lot – but he told me he got bonuses. I was very glad of the bonuses – obviously!

He carried on buying things without consulting me. I found it very annoying but he said he liked to surprise me. He bought everything for our house and had done from the first day – the kitchen units, the washing machine, he ordered the carpet for our bedroom (though he did ask me what colour I wanted at least). He often came home with stuff – another TV, a new set of cutlery, some pictures for the walls, various power tools (though he never used them). Masses of things, off and on all the time. One day he came home with a car load of designer clothes for me. I was thrilled. He explained that a client had gone in to liquidation and the he had bought the contents of the bankrupt boutique. Some of the clothes were too big or too small, but I gave them to my mum and my sisters.

Soon I found that I was expecting another baby. New furniture, carpets, a bigger car, car seats, a new buggy ...
Fin was out the day the police turned up. He was away seeing a client (or so I thought) and wouldn't be back till the following evening. I was over eight months' pregnant and I stood at the door slightly impatiently because whatever the police wanted, they had got the wrong house. Except they hadn't.

Fin was being held in custody. He was a professional burglar and he went down for fifteen years on twenty-five counts of breaking and entering, during which one person had been severely injured, and seventeen counts of fraud. He had been brilliant at it – he was proud of that – and had got away with it for many years. Almost everything in our house was stolen. Worse, it wasn't our house. It was rented and Fin had paid in cash every month.

The car and almost everything else was impounded. Along with my two daughters, then aged two and six weeks, I was evicted when I couldn't pay the rent and I went in to a one-bedroom flat. I felt totally dejected, and it was only because of my children I kept it together. You quickly learn who your friends are at times like that! Some of my so-called friends gloated. My mum was very supportive.

Fifteen years is a long time and I decided I would not wait for him. I know that sounds hard, and I tried to forgive him and side with him – but I couldn't. I wanted to move on. As soon as I had recovered from the shock of it all my decision was made. He had put himself in jail. The police (who actually were extremely kind) had questioned me, heavily pregnant and with a toddler at my side … Fin had no right to do that to me. All those times he told me he was seeing a client – well, he was on a job. The day Suzy was born he'd been stealing in a big mansion over by the lakes. All the lies!

When Fin gets out his girls will be big and they can look him up if they want to. Me, I do not visit him and I keep in touch only via his mother. I am not looking for a new man. I live on very little and am looking forward to going back to work as soon as the girls are old enough. South Africa is a big place and it is easy enough to disappear and start again, at least on the surface. It is still all very raw, and my new friends know nothing about it. That is why I have kept this anonymous.

David Bailey

Successful women

From Moira Trill

womenandbusiness.com.au

I have been asked to write an article about what makes a successful woman. The article should discuss a variety of dos and don'ts and cover the various elements of working onwards and upwards.

There are several books about this very topic already, though few devoted to the woman in this field. I puzzled for some time over how to approach the subject and, as I scribbled out my notes and bullet-pointed my ideas, it occurred to me that it would in many ways be better to discuss women who are not successful and why that should be.

Of course, there are plenty of women who trog along through life, perfectly content within their own limited spheres, and it doesn't occur to them to move onwards and upwards. Most people, male or female, are like that. And that is fair enough. Lots of women just want to be themselves and ask no more from life.

Mark you, there is not one who would object to having more money in their lives!

So I decided to take the example of three women I know quite well. Clearly I have to hide their identities, so for the purposes of this redaction, I will call them Avia, Jill and Mae. The names have just popped in to my head and (as far as I know!) are not their middle names or hide any other similar giveaway. I will just add that my aim here is not to bitch about other women, but simply to illustrate what I am saying.

Avia. Not a successful woman.

I was talking to Avia just the other day. She is a very part-time assistant in an art gallery (she is not, but that is close enough). She works one

and a half days a week, then four or five times a year she has to go in on a Saturday when there is an exhibition. Her two children have long since grown up and left home and she lives in a weeny (very pretty actually) house on the south coast of England with her partner.
She is not a successful woman. I have no idea if she ever wishes she were, or if she ever tried to be, but she is the epitome of the woman who is not, never has been, and never will be successful.

Avia has lived in the same town, or very close by, all her life. She enjoys walking and gardening and periodically produces a picture (oil, if memory serves) of ethnic-looking females or strange elongated characters. I quite like them, though I wouldn't want one hanging on my wall. The fact that she has virtually never set foot off the British Isles shows in these pictures – there is a lack of genuine feeling in them. They are pictures of what she thinks. Fair enough. As far as I am aware she has never sold one.

Avia thinks she is very busy. She is always telling me how busy she is. Yet she does nothing of any note, goes nowhere of any note, though I daresay she thinks she does. Now, perhaps that is unfair of me because it may well be that she has never aspired to be anything of any note. But that is not my point. My point is that she could not be, even if she wanted to – because you always find time to do the things you really want to do.

If you think you are too busy, you will not be an achiever. With the exception of a minority who are genuinely extremely busy – doctors perhaps, or farmers – you do always find time to do the things you really want to do. And if you really want to become a successful woman, you will find the time to do it.

The other thing that keeps Avia back is that she has no experience though, once again, she thinks she has. The truth of the matter is that she knows nothing about anything. She has got some half-baked qualifications in something arty (though qualifications are not necessarily of any use) and has lived all her life in a very narrow world, driving the same roads and meeting the same people. She has quite strong opinions which appear to be based on nothing much and she can be very judgemental about people, places and items. Which brings me on to another error people often make which is if you don't know what you are talking about, say nothing !

The trick, of course, is knowing when you don't know.

Jill. Almost successful but never quite there.

Jill is somebody I like very much indeed. She lives near Manchester with her husband and still has two teenage girls at home.

Jill has always been a grafter, has dipped her fingers in to lots of different pies, has travelled within Europe a fair bit, is bi-lingual, and willing to give it a go, whatever it is. She has been through the mill. She knows all about the dreadful pitfalls business can hold for us, the ups and downs and the joys and sorrows of deals and non-deals. But on her side she has experience, lots of it.

She does, however, make the same mistake as Avia and thinks she is too busy when she is not. She is indeed very busy, but a lot of her consumed time is because she is slow. She walks and moves very slowly. She writes an e-mail slowly. Her job involves her getting in and out of her car and this is also done excruciatingly slowly. As a result, she is fat. She never burns off calories. I estimate she loses at least two hours every day simply because she is so slow.

And this has a knock-on effect because you have to walk the walk
… and you have to look the look.

The nature of the business that Jill is in involves her clients needing to have great confidence in her. A crucial element of what she does requires her to look like a business woman, a successful woman, a woman who knows absolutely what she is talking about, who is on-the-ball, efficient and effective.

Jill does not look like this. She looks (bless her) more like a cariacature of a baker's wife. The tragedy is that she is in fact on-the-ball, efficient and effective. But it doesn't come over that way.

Oddly enough, her looks would work better for her if she decided to be eccentric. A dark business suit on her does her no favours, whereas in her boots I'd try colourful Indian-looking garb, or perhaps loud African prints, or at least or something rather more up-beat. She cannot hide that she is fat, so she should celebrate it. The sensible slacks with jacket just make her look fat and boring.

Jill needs to learn to move with alacrity, to speed up in every way, to dress to impress and to give her clients a feeling of "let's go!"
She does the very opposite.

Mae. Successful.

Mae lives in a pretty village in Devon with a teenager at home as well as her long-term partner and four dogs. She started her working life as a teacher. She went in to that profession for the long school holidays and the short hours. On the whole her job, however, was only moderately satisfying. From a very early stage Mae had a notion that she wanted more out of life – for herself and for her children.

More importantly, she determined that not only that she wanted to be rich but that she would indeed become rich.

It all depends, of course, on how you measure success. Mae could not possibly complete with the Alan Sugars and Richard Bransons of this world, and she wouldn't want to try. She knew, right from the start, what she wanted: a smart house and a smart car, holidays abroad at least once a year, being able to pay the bills without much of a fuss, being able to buy – within reason – most things she needs and wants; being in a position to contribute financially to those who need it and, on the whole, to be comfortable and happy. She focussed on this off and on for years, always taking a small step forwards and never allowing herself to fall back.

Mae's great assets are that she is energetic, speedy, positive and cheerful. And when you are energetic, speedy, positive and cheerful you find that opportunities somehow pop up around you. She and her family went through many traumatic situations where they were near to the depths of despair, but even in the darkest moments, Mae always looked out for the solution and told herself the one mantra that every successful person will agree with: get something out of this!

If nothing else, there is always a lesson to be learnt. The most dire situations can turn themselves in to an advantage – if you look for it.

I was sitting with Mae waiting for a flight once. The flight was at first delayed half an hour, then two hours, and finally five hours. Mae said to me "I am not sure what good can possibly come out of this, but I am sure there is something!"

I have no idea what positive aspect she found to that long, boring wait. However, her attitude summed her up. She is chatty, cheery, self-assured, knowledgeable, sharp, witty, flexible, determined and strong. And that is what has made her a success.

I am not going to give you a recipe on how to get rich, and I will send this very article to the editor of the magazine who asked me to write a "get rich" article. Because the trick to it is first of all to recognize what is keeping you back. You are perhaps keeping you back! The vast majority of people think they know more than they do (just listen to the people discussing politics at election time!) and, although self-confidence is a very good thing, it is also important to feel self-confident in the right way. Avia is self-confident, and that is nice for her, but she is self-confident over a nothing which is of no interest to anybody. Jill is also self-confident but holds herself back both physically and financially because she has not yet recognized that she must walk the walk.

Mae is supremely self-confident. She looks good (though I don't think she knows it), dresses smartly yet differently, speaks with a pleasant authority on lots of different subjects, has travelled a great deal all over the world (but this is since she became successful) and knows lots of things about lots of stuff. I remember her in her twenties (we were at University together) pouring over newspapers, which I found very boring.

"Whatever it is," she told me, "I want to know it."

For your notes:

- Feel like a winner. It is crucial to feel like a winner
- Concentrate on the passion and not on the money. Aim at what you desire, not at your bank account. The dosh will follow.
- You must have a total self-belief. Be really firm with yourself when you feel yourself wobbling
- Remember that success comes after many failures
- Remain in charge of everything. But delegate where appropriate. There is a real knack to knowing when to delegate and that took me a long time to get my head round – I felt I did it best, whatever it was

Felicity Banner-Brown

An X Chromosome
Dr Natally Alarab, Lebanon

"Never let go for your DREAMS"… and what will be better than such a quote to accompany me for a 6 years journey. That journey that has not even started yet…

From when I was 10 years old I was obsessed with reading. What have I read? Actually, all types of books have spent a night or more between my fingers, on my desk, or on my pillow. Although I have read a lot of autobiographies as well as biographies, I didn't imagine even for once that I would be writing my own and right now.

Oh sorry, excuse me ladies and gentlemen for I forgot to introduce myself. I am Natally. A 24 year old Lebanese girl, the oldest daughter of a 4-membered-family, a father, a mother, a younger brother and me. Despite of all the problems I have passed in during my childhood, I can still say that at least I have lived with the lowest standards of a peaceful life. It may be weird to talk about myself in this way but let us be clear from the beginning I now have the power to tell everything so why not utilize those moments.

I was what so called a NERD. That type of girl who never gets out of her house except to go to school. I used to visit some relatives like once per month and believe me the other ones I did not even know that they exist. My room was my kingdom. I was the queen and the books were my retinue. It is funny after all those years to have the courage to confess that I had a totally different whole new world in my imagination where I can find people that I can share with them my dreams, my ideas, my thoughts, what do I like and what do I don't. You may say that this seems insane but don't blame me. To live in a highly reserved society is not easy at all. The outer world was a monster to me. People where different creatures. I always had doubts if I was from another planet and I have landed to earth by mistake. The atmosphere at home was a little bit different. Yet my room was my only harbour in all that chaos surrounding my soul.

As I grew up that gap between me and the outer world began to widen more and more. My points of view never met theirs. Everything seemed different and my dreams became bigger and bigger and bigger. However, only one dream was conquering my mind in every step I make. Only one dream was the main reason behind that power that occupied me each time I wake up to mingle in that dead society-or to pretend I am- to go and fake that smile of happiness and return back home. It was all about entering medschool.

Flashback six years ago, I still remember that day when I was in the playground with one of my closest friends and that surprising look when she knew I want to be a doctor .

" …but Natally, you know you cannot ,it's so difficult and time consuming. How could you just think of spending 12 years studying Medicine. And… And have you forgot that you are GIRL!!!"

Of course some will be surprised of what they have just read, but others will not. Ironically to be born with XX chromosomes they have to let you pay the price without even taking your permission. It is funny that over all those years we have been teaching our kids that "X "means No or a symbol of a wrong thing and the tick means "right". Unfortunately, the magic turned on the magician or in other words all our illusions backfired on us. So be ready Eve, in your whole life you will be classified in the wrong list for your guilt is carrying the XX chromosomes. Congratulations!

What was pacifying me most of the time that my parents believed in me. And were always behind my back. Although the closest people and relatives were totally disagreeing about the idea of me studying medicine, my parents were always finding the right answers to all the peoples' ridiculous questions. One of the toughest moments that cannot be deleted from my memory was when one of my aunties told my father:

"Are you insane, why would you pay all those money on your daughter. It is your Daughter!! Can't you imagine what will happen after she finishes. She will go and marry and all the money you will spend on her will disappear in the air. Go and give the money to your son. At the end he will hold your name."

Silly principles are those that we are carrying in our heads, blood and milk; breastfeeding our infants irrational perceptions generation after generation. Sometimes I think of conducting a research about the origin of those thoughts and to know exactly if those odious standards are carried by our genes. What if we removed those traits would they reappear? Who knows may be a mutation will happen and they re-emerge. Maybe the secret lies in the water we drink or in the food we ingest or even in the air we inspire… I sometimes cannot imagine this society speaking other than those words. Unfortunately this language suits them the best…

June 2011 has come, I was standing in the middle of the playground holding my books in a hand and my handbag in the other hand shivering. I looked pale and scared with those black colour under my eyes. That was expected, I had not slept for nights. The bell rang, the voices around me started to rise. Some were laughing, others were complaining…but the only thing I was hearing were my heartbeats…I swear I had tachycardia. Ten minutes later I was in my seat, in front me my exam sheet and between my fingers my lucky pen.

"When I finish counting till three everyone will start solving in his /her sheet, no attempts of cheating are accepted or else he or she will be deprived of the exam," the supervisor said, " Good luck everybody ..1..2…3 start".

And the official exams started.

After 20 days or more I can't remember precisely

when the results were out .I have passed with a mention. All the family, relatives and friends greeted me. And the usual question was:

"What did you choose to study at the university?" ... and here comes the expected gaze when I say with mouthful:

"Medicine"!!

Here comes the second step, it is time to apply to the entrance exam for medicine school. Sometimes back at that days when all my friends were enjoying their vacation and I was in my room stuck with my books, I had that feeling of "What have you done stupid girl?" but then comes my mom with that wide smile to my room checking if I needed something with that sparkle in her eyes that says: "Yes you can do it!!"

That always gave the will to continue. However, there was something about my dad, something that I can't figure out. Something that kept me worried all the time .I can't deny that many times I was about to quit, nevertheless there was a special feeling from inside that always push me forward whenever I recall my first visit to my future university.

Three months ago it was like April, I was preparing for my finals at school when my father entered my room:

"Get up and put on your clothes, dear, we are going to a special place."

My heart was getting outside my chest once I knew it was the university I am going to apply to. Our undergraduate neighbour was waiting for us there since I was naïve in everything that has to do with the university requirements, credits , core courses, semesters and all those terms... funny yeah.

She was my supporting angel at that day and I was like a 3 years old kid looking at the people without understanding anything.

The university looked huge. Everything looked different. Even me, I looked different, I was calmer and all that energy inside me was curbed. As if it was a message that my destiny has something to do with this university. She introduced me to everything I should know at that stage, and I went home completely satisfied.

Two weeks after my preparations I did my entrance exam with full confidence, it was not easy at all. Everyone around me wasn't expecting me to be accepted. There was something new about it not to forget to tell you that I was the first member in my big family that applied to medicine school so how come they would accept it and I was a "Girl" , the first female doctor in the family. On the other hand my family was supporting me to the maximum.

My mom's eyes gave me always the power to believe in myself. Ten days later the home telephone rang I picked up the phone, it was dad...

"Congratulations darling, you have got accepted in medicine" ... all I remember at that moment is that I cried!

Yay I got accepted in medschool, I thought that the struggles have ended and I will raise the sign of victory until a new problem arrived. I was going to my living room with a wide smile holding my phone, the screen was displaying the accessed university website and what was the requirements of registration (it was manual in that days) when I heard my parents discussing my issue.

" ... but darling you know I don't have enough money, it is so expensive and I can't afford to pay the coming six years. It is too much to handle!"

Mom replied:

"I don't know! you have to do something about that, my daughter should enter the medical school in any way... I would sell everything to let her in. She was meant to be a doctor and she will be!"

I stood stunned at the door not knowing what to say or what to do. All what I was thinking about "is that the end of my dream"?!

Few days later I found myself at the university holding hands with my dad and with the other hand was a file containing all the required documents, photos, and medical laboratory tests. I don't know many details how things were settled at that period of time but what I know that my dad once entered my room, I was in tears. My father took me into his arms, smiled and wiped my tears away...

"Don't worry Natally everything will be alright, dear. Believe me everything will be alright". He smiled, I smiled back and kissed him on his forehead.

The first day of the university was hilarious. I looked like a 5 year-old girl going to the park for the first time. I was hyperactive, talkative and ready to understand a whole textbook in a single day. Believe me I don't know from where all that energy was coming from. I asked a lot and got questioned a lot. Day after day things where more difficult and confusing. A lot of burdens a lot of sleepless nights, a lot of disappointments and frustrations. Yet I was happy.

I had to meet a lot of people of different cultures and environments. Though Lebanon is considered one of the smallest countries in the world (10452 km^2), the cultures, way of thinking, and even the way of talking differs between the south, north, mount Lebanon, and the coast. Moreover, I had to spend some semesters away from home at the dorms so I can be near to my university since we had some clinics at night. All of those were limiting my abilities. Sometimes I even cannot doubt that I was thinking of quitting and maybe I would have done this if my parents weren't supporting me all the time.

In the second year of medicine school we had a cardiovascular-respiratory module. It was catastrophic. I spent a full day before my finals crying and weeping. My dad, my mom and my brother stayed the whole night calming me down, dad then looked at me and said:

"Don't you remember the day when we went for registration when we met those seniors what have you said ?! What happened to my little girl!"

I stopped crying, wiped away my tears and gave him a half smile. I remembered… that day when I was arriving at the elevator with my father, we have met senior medical students. From the papers we were holding it was clear that I was registering at the faculty of medicine they looked at me and smiled.

"So you are a junior little doctor," with a full smile.

"Yes, I am," and looked at my dad. He smiled back. One of the seniors replied:

" Oh little lady, you still have the chance to escape, medicine isn't fun at all. You are still young and of course you would not prefer to spend your whole years studying medicine…"

I frowned back and said:

"But I know what I am doing and I am happy choosing medicine".

They both looked at each other then looked back to me and said:

"Good luck, we have warned you and it is your choice". The elevator reached the ground floor and we all descended from it. I cannot deny that I went home with a full feeling of satisfaction and happiness that I was thinking that I would defeat the whole world to reach my goals.

A whole 6 years have passed with ups and downs, with nights of crying and others of laughter. With new people entering my life and others leaving it. Everyday passed was true evidence to all who said I can't reach my dreams. Thanks for those who told me once "No you cannot" so today I can stand in front of them and say "Yes I can" with all the power and determination I have earned. It was never getting easier but I was enduring more. Few months will come and I'll tell the whole world, here comes "

"If you obey all the rules, you miss all the fun."

Katharine Hepburn

Catherine Broughton

Exchanging time in your holiday home has real benefits

Carol Lintott

We've all heard of residential home swaps, thousands of people successfully exchange their residential homes with others every year. Now by using the same principle, there is a new small business helping holiday home owners exchange time in their holiday homes.

Passionate about travel, property and holiday homes in particular, Carol Lintott owns a holiday home in Southern England and a half share of an apartment in Southern Italy. Some time ago, a friend asked her if she would consider a holiday home exchange for a week. Thinking this was a smart way to use up empty weeks and get a holiday for just the cost of travel, she started to research the holiday home exchange market. Many searches later she had gathered information about what kind of offering was out there to bring together holiday home owners with a view to exchanging, the answer; very little! There were plenty of 'residential home' exchange companies, but only a couple of websites were found that catered solely for holiday home owners, and these sites seemed to have a complicated approach to exchange. The sharing economy is growing so Carol decided to create a simple web solution providing a platform for holiday home owners to showcase their properties and make contact with like-minded owners.

The ethos of MyHolidayHome.Exchange is therefore to keep it simple; one annual membership fee to join, no complicated points systems or 'banking' of weeks, just a straight forward exchange of time in each others properties with no other costs to pay.

The biggest challenge in setting the company up had to be the web design; the functional specification grew arms and legs, as did the timescale for delivery. But determined to make sure the website was right for launch Carol and her web designer battled on. The result is an interesting site, containing all the required member functionality, featuring secure messaging and an attractive property profile layout. Sourcing an Insurer and Marketing were the next big challenges, the latter Carol continues to work hard on.

A few reasons why holiday home exchanging is such a smart idea:
- There are no accommodation costs, saving a fortune on hotel bills
- Members get inside information on the location and the best places to visit from someone who knows the area as well as their home town
- Members get to visit other locations, using their holiday home as the key to new destinations
- Both holiday homes are already set up for holiday purposes
- Members make use of the time their holiday home would otherwise be sitting empty
- Members understand how holiday homes work, they treat each others place as they would their own
- Members can make new friends by connecting with other holiday home owners, maybe even arranging regular exchanges, a real holiday home from home!

At MyHolidayHome.Exchange all holiday homes are welcomed, from villas to houseboats. Even B&B owners can take advantage, using vacant nights in their business to take a well-earned holiday of their own. The administration side of membership management verifies all members by asking for photo identification and a copy of a utility bill for the holiday property in question.

Members do not have to take their exchanges at the same time, by communicating with their exchange partner, they arrange the exchange for a time when their holiday home will be vacant. Because members arrange their exchanges between themselves, there are no limits to the amount of exchanges each member can take, for just one annual membership fee, if they can arrange them, they can take them!

How Exchanges are arranged

Step 1: List the holiday home
Customers register as a member, adding a profile and their property details. The site recommends adding as much detail about the location, the property and its facilities as possible. To showcase the property the member uploads photographs. As mentioned earlier photo identification, a passport or driving licence, and a recent utility bill for the holiday home is also uploaded into a secure section of the site.

Step 2: Search for exchanges
Members begin by searching and drawing up a list of properties they are interested in. The site has the facility for a member to indicate destinations they would like to visit so members can narrow their list down by looking to see if there is a destination match. Next they open up the lines of communication using the sites secure messaging service.

Step 3: Connecting with other members
Initial messages do not commit a member to any exchanges, they are showing interest in another members holiday home and inviting them to talk about their property and whether an exchange would be possible. It is understood that further correspondence will be necessary before an agreement can be made.

Step 4: Organising the exchange
Once agreement has been reached, both parties are advised to complete an Exchange Agreement Form, the site offers a template for this and once completed they can commit to travel costs. There is usually much to talk about before an exchange and quite often exchange partners will be good friends by the time the exchange arrives.

Finally
Making a successful holiday home exchange requires some effort on the members part. Much of this effort for example, compiling an information folder, will be necessary for the first exchange only. Experienced exchangers know that making holiday arrangements becomes a very

simple routine. Holiday home exchanging is a trust based arrangement and as such, it tends to attract honest, trust-worthy, decent people. Exchange relationships are personal, not commercial and so there is a spirit of goodwill surrounding the arrangements. Good exchangers care as much about the comforts provided to their visitors as they do about their own.

About the Owner

My Holiday Home Exchange Limited was founded in September 2014 by Carol Lintott and she has now completed the first phase of development of the website. Carol's career started in banking in 1979, having undertaken various roles she left the bank in 2003. Since then she has undertaken a variety of contracts within the financial services industry mainly in Project Management. She is very involved in community work locally and continues to do the odd contract while running My Holiday Home Exchange.

twitter.com/MHH_E
facebook.com/myholidayhomeexchange

"A woman is like a tea bag. You never know how strong she is till she is in hot water."

- Eleanor Roosevelt

Kirsteen Lyons

Car crash

Sally Drake, Australia

Like with all these things, I assumed it would never happen to me.
I mean, you hear about it, don't you ? Every now and then you hear on the news about a car crash, sometimes you may even drive past one. When we drive past one we look in awe – a kind of morbid curiosity that we are all guilty of. In some ways it is amazing how few of us are in crashes.

Have you ever watched a film, sped-up, of vehicles on a road ? Logically, we should all crash far more frequently.

The night of my crash changed my life forever. It changed my job, my relationships, my values.

Yes, I'd had a couple of glasses of wine. Two actually. I had smoked a joint. One, just one. I had been at a party and, although it was not late (9.30) I was heading home because I was tired. I was an air-hostess. Was. It was a job I enjoyed but I won't pretend it was an all-encompassing career. I'd have preferred to keep the job, but it was okay that I didn't.

The point, however, is that it could have been devastating from the point of view of a career. I was just lucky.

So, anyway, that was three things counting against me before I even got in to my car. I had had a drink (two glasses of wine – nothing!), I had smoked a joint (shared with a friend – nothing!) and I was tired. Actually, I think it was the tiredness that did it. I didn't realize how tired until it was too late, and I think we are all of us slow to realize how tired we can be.

Oddly enough, the weather was against me too. It was a clear, mild, pleasant evening, with the faintest hint of a breeze, excellent visibility. Had it been raining, I'd have concentrated more.

My route took me down the road away from the party in a built-up area of Canberra. I swear I was not going fast. I felt slightly ratty because my boyfriend had stayed at the party – I had been away on flights to the USA and back all week, and I felt he should have preferred to be with me. Even so, I swear I was driving sensibly.

So why did I veer off the road in to a tree ?

I was aware that I was tired and was looking forward to getting back to my flat. The following day I was to have lunch with my mum and sister who both lived – as I now do – in Brisbane. I have no recollection of feeling specifically sleepy and I have no recollection of something (an animal?) making me jump, nor of something else (turning on the radio? Adjusting the mirror?) making me lose concentration.

I just suddenly found myself upside-down in my car. There were lots of banging sounds, extremely loud. I was conscious of huge noises and, stupidly, I thought a bad storm had started. You know how you can think a whole paragraph in a split second? Well, it crossed my mind that the thunder sounded odd, not like normal thunder, and that is was very close.

Several minutes went by before I was able to work out that I had crashed. The noises stopped and everything became eerily quiet. I was annoyed, and surprised, but not frightened. I was relieved that I wasn't injured, and I was concerned about the garage bill for damage to my car. I was aware that the car had turned over and that I needed to get out. I think I even said something like "oh shit!" and started to work out how to extricate myself from my strapped-in upside-down position.

As I tried to move I realized that one of my legs seemed to be caught on something, or pinned under something. I couldn't feel it at first, then, a bit at a time, a massive pain crept in, searing up all over my leg, a pain so huge that I – still relatively calmly – assumed it was broken.

I looked out of the upside-down window and I could see people moving. Two men. I was glad they were there. They would open the door, unhook my leg from whatever it was caught on, and haul me out.

I called out. I heard one of them respond – it's all right, we're here ! That voice sounded wonderful to me.

I'm not sure at which stage I realized the car had caught on fire. At least five minutes must have gone by. I could hear sirens as the police approached, and then I became aware of a smell … acrid smoke, petrol, the smell of heat. Most of all the smell of fear.

Until that moment I was not afraid. I am (was) a logical sort of person. I didn't think this in sentences (so to speak) but my overall thoughts were that it was an infernal nuisance about the car, that broken legs heal and – stupidly – I even thought about getting several weeks off work!

I couldn't understand why nobody had fished me out of the car yet and, as I realized about the fire I started screaming at the men outside to get me out. I also started to feel very sick (I was upside down, after all!) Something sticky had got in to my eye and suddenly all of me hurt terribly. Really bad pain – everywhere. Pain as bad as the worst moments of childbirth – except that it was everywhere.

The worst was the smell of my own leg burning. When I realized what it was, that was the worst.

After what seemed like a very long time somebody – an ambulance man – pushed through one of the windows and got a drip in to my arm. He was saying something about pain. His voice was reassuring but brisk. I wanted him to pick me up and hug me till I felt better. I wanted to cry and cry. I kept saying "get me out, get me out" and he (I think it was him) kept replying "we're working on it".

By the time they had started cutting away parts of my car I was drifting in and out of consciousness. I could see a lot of smoke, and white foam covering areas all around me. My mobile rang and in my fuzzy state I was upset that I couldn't answer it and I tried to say something to one of the rescue workers about answering my phone for me. I could hear my own voice making bizarre mmmm sounds, and felt very grateful that I seemed to be going to sleep.

I came to again in the hospital. These were my injuries:

- Left leg: both tibia and fibia broken
- Right leg: broken in several places, 3rd degree burns from my foot to just above my knee, huge lacerations, a metal shaft through the calf. The leg was amputated.
- Three broken ribs
- Large cut on forehead, required 18 stitches
- Right shoulder discolated
- Right lung pierced: it was collapsed (yes, I use just one lung now)
- Multiple fractures and cuts

My injuries were such that when I learnt that Davey, the boyfriend, had met somebody else at the party and had gone home with her I didn't much mind. It was the least of my problems. In fact, he didn't know anything about the crash for four or five days. He came to see me on the fifth day, carrying a bunch of inexpensive flowers. I cried a lot.

The next weeks were sort-of white. I know that is a funny thing to say, but in my mind everything seems to be white and misty. Sometimes I came to properly and the pain was dreadful. I was aware of nurses (such amazing people!) clearing up my shit and changing dressings and trying to say reassuring things to me.

Both my parents and my sister were there every day. They kept saying things like "you are strong, you will get over this" – and I knew that to be true.

Being fitted and learning to use my prosthetic leg – about a month later - was excruciating. It was hard work and I can well understand people who give up on it. It took 8 weeks. Actually, I mind the scar on my forehead more. It goes right across and is still very red. I am looking in to plastic surgery, but I am not sure if I can stand more hospital.

If anybody reading this feels sorry for me – well, don't. My recovery was painful, especially with the artificial leg – that took me seven months to get properly used to! – but I did recover.

Sure, there were times I felt I would never get over the shock and that I would never get used to only having one leg, but mostly I was positive. My parents and my sister were very supportive and they never treated me as "poor Sally" in any way.

Now ? Six years have gone by. I met and married a gorgeous man two years ago, and we have a baby daughter. I never returned to work with the airline, but they covered almost all my medical and rehabilitation expenses. Before I got married I worked part-time in a little florist's near my flat. Although I won't pretend I actually like my fake leg – I don't mind it either. People get used to these things very quickly. I have the big scar on my forehead, and the rest of me healed.

You do recover, you know. Life even goes back to normal in many ways. If something like this has happened to you or to somebody you love – know this: you do recover.

www.flyingdoctor.org.au
www.australianroadsafetyfoundation.com

Catherine Broughton

My husband has Meniere's Disease
Gilly Tamlin, UK

Many people have never heard of Meniere's. But, like so many of these things, once you have it you find you meet people with it, or people who know somebody with it, off and on all the time.

Meniere's is an inner-ear illness named by a Frenchman, Prosper Meniere in 1861. Its main symptoms are dizziness, tinnitus, headache and deafness.

The difference between the disease and the syndrome is that the syndrome can be related to a particular factor, e.g stress, that causes the discomfort and can often, therefore, be cured.

The disease is when the cause is unclear and there is no cure. It steadily gets worse. Both the syndrome and the disease can be extremely unpleasant and can vary hugely from one day to the next. Both can last for many years, even a lifetime. Both can be utterly debilitating.

My husband has Meniere's disease. It started to manifest itself some twenty years ago when he developed a buzzing sensation in his head. He also had a sensation of an extra body of some kind under his skull and I recall him telling me that he felt as if there was a heavy wet sponge there; then suddenly the heavy wet sponge would go very dry and brittle, then wet again. He wondered off and on if he had an ear infection because one ear seemed to be sometimes painful and sometimes – again – that sensation of there being something in it.

The weeks drifted by and the discomfort got no better. We noticed that he seemed to have difficulty hearing, particularly on one side. Not only had his hearing deteriorated but he couldn't tell where the sound was coming from, not even from his good ear. At one stage a bird in the garden up in a tree seemed to him to be louder than my voice right next to him. That kind of thing.

Again, the sensation of dizziness just puzzled us, when that started. Low blood pressure ? Did you stand up too quickly, perhaps? Have you hit your head ? Perhaps you've got a cold coming ?

When the dizziness didn't go away we went to the doctor who diagnosed Meniere's. He was referred to an ear specialist who could do nothing for him.

Since then my husband has tried all sorts of medications, both chemical and "natural", acupuncture, reflexology, massage ... the lot. Nothing so far has solved the problem. There are times, which may last weeks on end, where the only discomfort he has (and he has these permanently, day and night) are tinnitus in varying degrees of volume, deafness and an inability to make any sudden movements because it will trigger dizziness (looking left and right when driving for example – he always thinks-out this movement). He is also permanently unable to tell where a sound is coming from. Then there are times, often weeks on end, when he feels so sick and dizzy that all he can do is lie down. Sometimes he lies on the floor because he says he cannot fall off the floor. Sometimes he is sick. Sometimes his headache is so bad that nothing seems to alleviate it.

He has been hospitalized with the illness and at one stage spent almost ten months in bed – not non-stop, but he remained in bed most of the day, most days. He felt utterly wretched. It also made him depressed. And yet he is one of the lucky ones! Many have vastly greater discomfort.

We have noted a few things that help/make it worse:

- Total peace and quiet lying in the sun is very helpful
- Noisy places make it worse
- High-pitched noises (a chair scraping on the floor for example) can be out-and-out painful
- He needs people to talk gently WITH him rather than AT him

- Oddly enough white sugar seems to make it worse
- He can drink only decaffeinated tea and coffee, and those only in small quantities
- Cheese will trigger an attack, though goat's cheese in small quantities seems to be OK
- Even a stressy item on the TV seems to be unhelpful
- Having a cold is devastating for him. We all know that most men make the most inordinate fuss when they have a cold (bless), but a cold mixed with Meniere's is very bad news in this house
- Flashing TV or cinema images, anything in that line (the lighting in the aquarium triggered an attack), moving lights
- Massage seems to help
- Some forms of Yoga help
- migraine - we found that he sometimes has a migraine (as opposed to a headache) with the attack, and this part can be easily resolved with Zomig
- Xanax is helpful at night or when the attack means you must lie down
- travel sickness tablets sometimes help
- oxygen is sometimes extremely helpful though the doctor says this is illogical

These are all things that Meniere sufferers are long familiar with. There is no cure. The worst causes of the illness, whether the syndrome or the disease, seems to be stress and loud noises.

Your best help and advice will come from other Meniere sufferers, not from your doctor. The illness has been identified, which is not the same as being understood. There are lots of web sites where you can exchange information with others .... and it will make you realize that you are in fact very lucky that yours is not so bad that it prevents you from reading this blog! Here are a few words from him:

"On the days that you feel all right, it is essential that you do your best to carry on with your normal life, even if the tinnitus is bad. I find that if I immerse myself in what I am doing (providing it is not something that will trigger an attack!) I can almost forget the tinnitus and headache.

I keep myself very busy so that I do not dwell on it and, oddly, I stopped reading so much about it because I found it quite discouraging to know how bad it could get! Always avoid loud noise and rushed movements. I do not talk about the disease with other people because I do not want constant sympathy and I do not want to focus on it.

However if there is somebody talking very loudly at me (almost always a woman!) I do tell them. The best possible thing for me is peace and quiet, sunshine, and feeling generally at ease with the world."

www.menieres.org.uk

Interview with Sarah Bailey-Williams

1) Tell us a bit about who you are

My name is Sarah and I am a 45 yr old mother of three girls, a sexual abuse survivor, a wife, and a hard working PA!

2) As a woman in a man's world, do you have any particularly strong opinions about women's rights and the role of women in our society?

I believe the role of women in our society is greatly under-estimated. I believe that not only are we under-estimated but we under-estimate ourselves! I find it appalling that there are still many fields where earning potentials for women are so much less than that of men.

3) Would you say it is a man's world?

Yes SADLY! Advancement is easier for men, partly because society is conditioned (even now) to think of men as the main earner and also because men have more ease of movement through the world. However, I do recognize that the role of women has changed for the better in lots of ways over the last 100 years.

4) Are there any big changes that could be made for women in western society?

Bring wages in all areas in line and not gender related.

5) What have been your greatest joys?

My Children, my grandchildren

6) Is there a woman in history you particularly admire?

Princess Diana, I truly believe that she has made a really positive impact on our country and monarchy, and showed love. She also made some silly judgements which ensured we remembered she was human!

7) Do you have a favourite female author?

There are several I like:
Jojo Moyes, Catherine Broughton, Linda Laplante, and a few others.

8) Do you have an opinion about Page 3 girls and similar?

Good luck to them if they make a living over men being boys!!!

9) You have three daughters - do you see them secure as women?

I hope so. I have always tried to instil the right values in them.

10) Tell us something surprising about you

My eldest daughter used me (unknowingly) in court to avoid prosecution and this resulted in my being arrested! As a result I spent the night in a cell as we had to wait for a duty solicitor. I had my finger prints taken and DNA swabs and the humiliation of peeing in a bucket!!!!

At the time wondered how I would ever move forward and have a relationship with her again (I had never been in trouble with the police and was petrified.) Needless to say I had done nothing wrong and was released. But 5 years on she and I have a good relationship - (it never truly leaves the back of my mind, however a mothers love finds a way!!)

Kirsteen Lyons

"When she transformed in to a butterfly, the caterpillars spoke not of her beauty but of her wierdness. They wanted her to change back into what she had always been.

But she had wings."

- Dean Jackson

Interview with Balcita Blue

1) First, tell us a bit about who you are and what you do

I am not your average All-American 16 going on 17 kind of girl. My mother is not Susie-Homemaker and my father is not an everyday working man. I spent most of young childhood living homeless on the streets of South Lake Tahoe with my mother; even once having to live in a box on my own behind a Taco-Bell. My father, well, I never knew him because he spent most of his life memorizing the cold-cracks of a prison wall. I've made many mistakes in my life and I've lived to regret them all. But, one thing my life has taught me is to learn to live with my mistakes and make a little bit of difference in my corner of the world. Consequentially, in despite of my past, I've championed to help the hungry, became a dyslexic tutor, a social-change author, and the CEO of the upcoming corporation Balcita Enterprise, LLC.

2) What do you feel passionate about and why?

I feel passionate about homeless people because I once was homeless, hungry, and afraid, feeling like a ghost fading into the whispers of the wind. I am glad to have lived like them. Because, it taught me that behind the dirt, grime, booze, and banality of "the banes of society," lies a person with a bleeding heart-a feeling soul-dying to tell their story to the world. Begging people to know that they've existed. That they were here and LIVED. My passion of helping the homeless has led me into pursuing a career in the F.B.I so that I may be a voice for the people who have no hope and can't speak for themselves.

3) You were once homeless - can you tell us a bit about that?

My mother went a little crazy and thought the Russian Mafia was after her---she also was a prostitute, fugitive from the law, drug-addict, and alcoholic. What this led to was her getting tired of my presence, handing me five dollars and wishing me good-luck in the world, and her not enrolling me in the Eighth-Grade. Consequentially, I became an autodidactic learning languages, mathematics, literature, history, and much more, which led me into graduating high-school at 16. What haunts me the most about the past is the feeling of hunger; it is nearly indescribable. However, it kept me so much company that I know that feeling all too well. Hunger...Hunger is like a claw resting in the middle of your stomach, and as time ticks away the claw slowly...ever so slowly... closes, and as it closes it scrunches your insides. Once you experience true hunger it is almost near impossible to alleviate. And the ghost of it.... of hunger.... lives inside of you for as long as you live.

4) You are a writer - what is your genre?

I wouldn't say I am a writer or a poet. The world is filled with writers and poets ranting at things they cannot do or understand. No, I would say that I am an Author, yes, but I am more simply a person who has walked a road less travelled by and has a story to tell. All ten of my books do not fit into genres; they're non-classifiable. Mainly, the purpose of my books is to affect a social-change and make a difference in someone's life.

5) What are your 5 most favourite things?

1. Charles Bukowski; He is a man who has walked the same life I have, makes true poetry, and has enough substance and externals to know the truth about life's ordinary madness.
2. My grandfather Michael Lee Griffis; He was a person that I will never forget. I loved him so dearly that I strive to show his kindness and gentleness in everything I do.
3. My high-school diploma; My high-school diploma symbolizes everything I have accomplished in my life.

4. A letter from Noam Chomsky; When I was 14 Chomsky wrote to me and told me I would be wonderful in ivy-league school and have major success in life. I wrote to him to tell him how much I enjoyed his piece on Anarchism.

5. A photograph of my grandfather and I; The photo reminds me of a simpler time when innocence was all I knew.

5) and least favourite?

1. Ignorance; Ignorance may be bliss but knowledge is power.
2. People who say they don't read; I have no words past that.
3. Cellphones and television; They're the death of the human race.
4. Republicans; They're just so......
5. Religion; Imagine all of the people living for today!

7) Writers are often arty people - does this apply to you? Music? Art?

I find beauty in Bach and Mozart and the art of writing and the art of adventure in reading a good book.

8) If and when you have a daughter what do you consider to be the most important thing to teach her?

I do not intend to have children. Having lived the life I did, there is no way I'd want to bring a child into this fast-paced rat-race in a haze of consumerism.

But, if I did have a daughter I'd tell her this: The world is fast-paced. Black. Wrong and twisted. Have hope. For hope will get you through anything, and love---love the people who'll bring you down, and most importantly, love the people who will tell you that you can't do anything because you're a girl, and then, SHOW THEM UP!

9) Name a woman in history you admire - and why.

This is impossible to say I admire only one woman--I admire many. Like Sojourner Truth, Abigail Adams, Gloria Steinem, Alice Walker, Suzan B. Anthony, Elizabeth Cady Stanton, Margaret Fuller, Mala, Lydia Cannan, Kate Sheppard, Ayaan Hirsi Ali, and the list goes on.

I admire these amazing women because throughout history they fought the patriarchy, stood up to the status quo, and said we don't give a damn to what a woman should do. But, most of all I admire my grandmother Brenda Carole Holt. She saved me from the life I was living and taught me what it means to be a strong woman.

10) Tell us something surprising about you.

At 16-years-old I convinced a group of white tawdry men to invest over $500,000 into my idea of a company.

And, it worked.

The minute I turn 18 my company will go live and I'll be named the CEO of Balcita Enterprise, LLC and Balcita Publishing House.

145

Catherine Broughton

Published by
atlapublishing.com

Other books:

The Flyleaf Chronicles
Kefani
Short Stories and Tall Tales
Stories in Green Ink
Poetry without Borders
The Foodie Book
A Call from France
The Man with Green Fingers

Printed in Great Britain
by Amazon